EDUCATION TODAY

Projects in the Primary School

Projects in the Primary School

EILEEN M. HAGGITT

Lecturer in English
Bordesley College of Education
Birmingham

LONGMAN

LONGMAN GROUP LTD LONDON
*Associated companies, branches and representatives
throughout the world*

© Longman Group Ltd 1975

First published 1975
ISBN 0 582 32093 3

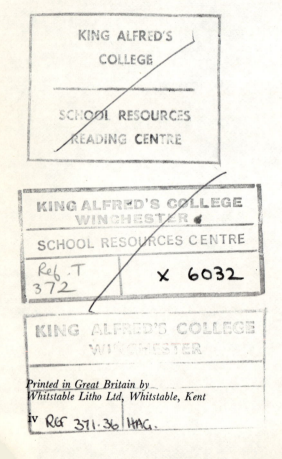

*Printed in Great Britain by
Whitstable Litho Ltd, Whitstable, Kent*

iv RGF 371.36 HAG.

Contents

Introduction

In this book projects are described as they developed in practice. The age ranges given are arbitrary. In my experience, children introduced to a spread of work around a theme will themselves indicate how sophisticated that work can be in its various aspects. Teachers will know best the attainment and ability of each individual in a class. A child making a start on a piece of research will reveal what he knows, what he needs to know, and what he is ready to learn. The teacher can then step in with individual teaching, or supplement the work in projects with class lessons on specific topics. I have found that project work offers immediate reasons for learning certain techniques and that children are therefore more receptive to the teaching of these techniques at this time. Like circular ripples from a stone dropped in a pool, too, ideas introduced at one stage can be expanded at a later stage, and further developed at a later stage again.

A theme is a central idea. A project is the spread of work across the curriculum that stems naturally from that idea. I have found that a good method of making an initial plan around a theme, is to note down the ideas which *immediately* spring to mind around the theme. The chances are that the connections one sees are those most logical to the children too. Thus:

TREES—leaves, trunks, shade, height. This preliminary plan can then be expressed in terms of appropriate recording. Thus:

Leaves—leaf—prints (craft) related shapes (art and mathematics) growth (nature study) decay (soil study).

Trunks—bark (rubbings—craft) height and girth (mathematics) growth (nature study) creatures that live in the bark (nature study).

Shade—spread (mathematics) shadows (science).

Height—(mathematics) use of trees for building etc. (social studies) comparisons.

Trees generally—pleasure (expression) appearance (expression) use, when growing and when felled (social studies) famous trees in history and Bible stories, adventures in trees.

It is important to keep project work compact and contained so that there is an overlap of activity, ideas and vocabulary. This overlap gives project work its coherence. Thus the theme: 'The sea' is too vast an area of study to be tackled at one time. It would be more profitable to explore one of the following in depth: 'Britain's seashore', 'Coral islands', 'Sailing ships', 'Sea monsters', 'Trawling', 'The tides'. I see project work as involving the whole class on a common theme: the projects developed were designed to give unstreamed classes a common purpose and to give individuals opportunities for contributing at their own levels.

Themes throw up opportunities for practising old techniques, and teaching and learning new ones. No one theme provides an equal amount of work in each of the disciplines. Most themes have a bias towards one or two disciplines to the neglect of others. Themes followed over three terms can be chosen to provide for adequate acquaintance with all the subjects on the timetable through project work. In schools where teaching through themes can only occupy some of the time, the method can still be used to introduce or reinforce teaching undertaken in other ways. In my opinion the claim of project work to be included in the timetable is fivefold. It gives a common purpose to an unstreamed class, it acts as a springboard for the teaching of techniques, it provides interesting experiences within the classroom as a basis for expressive work, it is a sharing of experience, and it provides children with goals towards which they can make genuine (if limited) choices.

All project work provides a continuum of learning and practice in using language (both oral and written), seeing and expressing relationships, sharing ideas, books, space, equipment, in organizing information and recording appropriately. Its emphasis is on learning to find out and to record what is found out, and in expressing experiences gained rather than in amassing facts.

Project work does not imply wholly group-based activities. The method of teaching and the size of group is that which is appropriate to the material to be taught. Class lessons enable teachers to supplement children's own research, to teach and remind children of techniques, and to collate activities. Group-based work is appropriate to situations where the children are exploring or experimenting with material and ideas. It allows children to discuss among themselves and to help one another. Individual work is appropriate for expressive writing and painting and for practice.

It is not necessary for all children to cover all assignments individually in every project. If children are working in an atmosphere of sharing they will watch, discuss and know what others are doing and finding out. A series of themes with well-structured project work will give all children, over three terms, an adequate share of all the opportunities available.

When a teacher is planning work round a theme, he will be aware of sequences of activities that can be undertaken and of the general concepts the children will be acquiring. The teacher's records should show how children are moving through a sequence of activities and also what concepts they are acquiring. Thus a record of free-writing should contain an objective assessment of the child's progress after consideration of every piece of writing offered by the child (or of a series of strategically chosen pieces offered throughout the year). Children's progress through a sequence of concepts in mathematics (e.g. linear measurement) can be recorded under such headings as: estimation, use of non-standard measurements, use of standard measurements, recording in words, recording in symbols, comparisons in words, comparisons in symbols, e.g. 6 metres—4 metres=2 metres, adding by multiplying, averages, i.e. division, and so on. Teachers will want to keep records of reading progress (where projects provide practice) and comprehension (research requires and tests comprehension). These records will probably be from results obtained from regular standardized tests.

There are themes where work starts from research in books and themes where work starts from direct observation. The former include themes where the work has a bias towards history or geography of other lands. I call these vicarious experience projects and feel that elements should be included to help children to be directly involved in an imaginative way. Drama, expressive writing and painting, and model-making help here. Children making a model of a Viking longship not only begin to imagine themselves sailing in it but find that the activity informs their pleasure in stories about Vikings. The latter projects, those starting from direct observation, include field studies and themes with a bias towards science. Here the children start by recording observations, asking questions that are explored by experiment and then turn to books for additional information.

Teachers know about teaching. They are not expected to know everything about every subject covered in project work. I find it helpful to regard myself as a learner with the children. There is a wealth of reference material available to both teachers and children. The information contained in Primary reference books is helpful to teachers too. I recognize two kinds of reference books of use in a Primary classroom: those that can be used by the children themselves without help (although here one must be wary of material that distorts the facts in order to simplify), and those which can be used profitably with some help from the teacher. The latter are those books where the reading content is difficult but where the illustrations are clear and informative (Methuen's Outlines and Burke's Young Specialist Books are cases in point). In the book lists that follow descriptions of project work, I have categorized books as follows:

I. *Infant*: simple reading content, clear pictures (can be used profitably by Juniors on their own, too).

I/J. *Infant/Junior*: books that can be used by Infants with teacher's help and by Juniors on their own.

J. *Junior*: books to be used by Juniors who can read and comprehend well.

J/T. *Junior/Teacher*: books to be used by top Juniors, Middle School pupils and less able Juniors with teacher's help.

T/J. *Teacher/Junior*: books of more help to teachers than to pupils.

T. *Teacher*: adult reference books.

Children should be encouraged to make notes from several books on the same topic rather than to follow slavishly one book or an encyclopaedia reference. The practice of making notes is a specialized technique and can be taught (for instance: notes are not necessarily in complete sentences; a labelled diagram is often an efficient way of jotting down information from books). The idea that a transactional book is not read from cover to cover should be stressed and children encouraged to make use of indexes for quick reference.

This book does not need to be read from cover to cover either. I hope teachers will look at themes which interest them and adapt the work described to suit their needs.

The work cards described in this book are not designed to provide assignments in which the children can work without help. They are designed as starting points only for the children and as opportunities for teaching when the children have made a start.

In the last analysis, it is the teacher's own genuine enthusiasm and interest which will guarantee the success of project work. The teacher must be as interested as the children in finding out, sharing ideas, exploring, discussing and recording results.

Theme work is hard work. It needs insight, organization and continuing enthusiasm. But in fifteen years of teaching in this way, I have found it rewarding, satisfying and a 'natural' way of teaching and learning. And, it seems to me, the continued emphasis in project work on sharing, can be only of benefit to the community at large of which the children are potential members.

I

Theme: The Milkman

This project was carried through with a class of thirty-two infants, aged five plus to six. There was a wide range of ability. Reading ability in the class fell into four main stages: non-starters, word readers, phrase readers and children recognizing words and phrases in several different contexts. Ability in mathematics ranged through one to one matching, matching groups of objects to number symbols, some idea of addition and subtraction in concrete terms. Some children were coming to terms with concepts of size, and the ability to categorize using various criteria: colour, size, shape and so on. Some children had an emerging concept of conservation.

The children were used to a procedure whereby they were given time to discover and experiment through 'play', and later were led, by specific questions from the teacher, to more contained and particular discoveries. At this stage they were encouraged to record their discoveries in words and in mathematical symbols.

Ability to write freely could be described under four main headings: non-starters, those who could tell the teacher what they wanted to say (the teacher wrote this down for these children to copy), those beginning to frame sentences for themselves, and those who could put together several reasonably coherent statements. The children were encouraged to write about their activities and to make labels for their work on display. The children drew pictures first and then, in discussion with the teacher, wrote about the pictures. The practice of drawing pictures before writing helped children to formulate and order their subsequent 'compositions'.

The teacher had brought in a picture of a milkman delivering milk. The children were able to tell the teacher how often milk was delivered to their homes, the name of the basket used for carrying milk and why the milkman needed a van to carry his deliveries. The teacher told them that the van was called a 'float' and that it was designed to run quietly and smoothly along the road. Peter, whose father was a milkman, offered to find out more about milk floats: the greatest speed at which they could operate, what kind of engines they had, how many crates they could carry and so on. There were two major milk companies serving the area. The teacher had an empty milk bottle belonging to each company and showed the children the name of the company embossed on the bottle. The children commented that tops of milk bottles were of different colours and in order to find out more about this, the teacher suggested they make a collection of milk bottle tops. Two boys offered to draw the milk floats used by each of the companies. The children were then directed to groups.

The teacher in this class allowed children to choose their activities from a range, put out for them on tables, but where too many children chose one activity, she directed some to another. In most groups the maximum number was seven, but in the painting corner the limit, because of space, was four children.

This procedure of allowing children to choose activities is followed in many Infant classrooms. It means that all activities must be made equally attractive and that the teacher must be prepared to use the children's immediate interests to develop learning along a broad front. The use of a theme to link activities means that the ideas and vocabulary around those activities overlap at certain points and that these activities contribute to a common goal.

The classroom had, in permanent use, a painting corner, a book corner, a table for writing activities, a water tray, a sand tray, a corner for woodworking and junk modelling and a clay table. The teacher saw that the clay and sand activities would not be very profitable in the initial stages of this theme and so these were covered. At the water table, she removed some of the utensils (a sieve and some lemonade bottles) but left funnels, plain jugs, graduated jugs and the two pint milk bottles together with a school milk bottle.

The teacher left a group of children here to experiment with the equipment provided. Later she suggested that the children find out whether the two tall milk bottles held the same amount of liquid. She left the children with this problem, returning later to discuss with them how they had tackled it. She left them again with two new problems: (1) to find out how many times they would have to fill the half pint measure to have the same amount of liquid as could be contained in one tall milk bottle; and (2) to find a jug that would hold exactly as much liquid, as one of the tall milk bottles.

The children in this group got out the poppet beads. The teacher suggested they arrange the beads like bottles in a crate. She asked them to discover whether the crate in the picture (now on the wall) held as many bottles as the crate which held the school milk bottles. Later she returned to help with this problem. She suggested that the children put a poppet bead on top of every bottle in the school milk crate. Then the beads were collected again and counted. Someone else counted the bottles. The children then took a poppet bead for each section in the crate in the picture. This crate was found to have less sections than the crate in the classroom. 'How many less?' asked the teacher and went away. She came back to find that an answer had been arrived at. The children had compared the two strings of beads which represented sections in each crate. The teacher showed the children how to record their discovery in symbols $36-12=24$, and suggested that they record what they had discovered in words. The children drew a picture of themselves finding out and pictures of the two crates and the teacher helped them to write sentences underneath their pictures. The completed papers were pinned on the wallboard under the picture of the milkman.

Meanwhile Jenny was painting, as she always did, a house. The teacher suggested that Jenny paint a milk float calling at the house and the milkman delivering some milk. When Jenny had done this the teacher asked her how many bottles the milkman delivered daily to her house. She replied 'Two', and the teacher wrote under Jenny's painting: 'The milkman is delivering two bottles of milk at Jenny's house.' Jenny copied this to make a label for her painting. She also wrote underneath: 'I like milk'. The painting and Jenny's label went up on the wall.

Bobby painted a picture of himself drinking some milk and the teacher suggested he put some jugs and mugs on the table in the picture. When the teacher returned to Bobby they evolved a label for the picture which read: 'There are two mugs and one jug on the table. Bobby is drinking milk. He is using two straws.'

At the painting corner the children learned not only to handle paint and make large graphic movements, to make choices about brushes, colours and ways of applying the paint, but they learned that painting is only one way of expressing an idea. Sometimes writing, modelling or mathematical recording may also express aspects of the same idea. The problem with children painting is often: 'What to paint?' Themes offer subjects for painting, and discussion about a theme and discoveries made in other activities may help to 'inform' the painting. Of course it is not always necessary to have a subject for a painting. Children love exploring the nature of the medium itself and there should be opportunity in school for them to do so, but for many children, especially inexperienced writers, graphic art is a way of expressing an idea or telling a 'story'. Children learn later that ideas may be expressed in different ways and that painting is only one of them. Jenny may paint a house every time because she wants to, or because she was once praised for painting a house, or because she feels unable to paint anything else, or because she does not know what else to paint. The current theme may provide her with further ideas. Bobby is telling a story in his painting. The teacher shows him that he can also tell a story in words. Later she may be able to demonstrate that words will describe what a picture often cannot: quality of movement, for instance, or the feelings of the participants.

In the book corner the children found one reference book about milkmen and several about cows. The teacher suggested they could find out how milk gets to their own houses from farms. Eventually they made a frieze showing first a cow, then a churn, then a milk container truck on a train, a milk float, a bottle of milk and a picture of themselves drinking milk. A frieze can act as the record of a group response in which ideas in sequence can be worked out pictorially. This kind of investigation precedes sequential, ordered, written accounts. Sentences under each of the pictures, when put together, tell the 'story' as a narrative.

At the junk modelling table children were trying to make milk floats. They encountered the perennial problem of making wheels. One child had cut circles of card but these were not strong enough to support his float. The teacher discussed this problem with the group. 'What are wheels for?' she asked. The children replied that they were for carrying the vehicle along. They would need to be placed so as to hold the vehicle off the ground, they would need to be strong enough to do so and they would need to turn smoothly. The teacher showed the children that a book pushed along a desk moves more easily and smoothly if it is supported by two round pencils. She then left the children with the problem but brought some pieces of dowel and some cotton reels to the modelling box. Later, when one boy had finished his model, he wanted to write the name of the dairy company along the side. The teacher showed him how to make a rubbing of the embossed wording on a milk bottle. When this rubbing was trimmed it was stuck on the side of the model milk float. The modellers cleared away their materials and went to the writing table to draw and write about what they had been doing.

In this classroom the writing table provided a clean space where children could write about their other activities. A supply of paper, crayons, pencils and spirit markers was available nearby. The teacher encouraged the making of labels for the resulting products of other activities. She pointed out that although a child could talk to some of his friends about what he had done, when his work went on display he might not be near at hand to explain it orally. Then his written explanation would do the telling for him. The teacher kept a box of flashcards containing words from the basic word list of the reading scheme in use in the class, and supplemented by flashcards of words suggested by various themes. The children used these flashboards to help them with spellings.

Assessment

Group activity periods like these usually lasted, with the preliminary discussion, for one half of a morning or afternoon session. In these periods the teacher moved from group to group using the children's activities as a basis for conversation and teaching. Her function was to suggest and develop. The theme gave her a point of reference with each group.

The walls of the classroom reflected the growth of the project. They also provided a means of communicating ideas throughout the class. When the teacher came to write her records of each child's progress (at this school this was done daily) work displayed on the wall reminded her of what children had done.

The keeping of records is an important part of any teaching situation and needs to be kept up carefully in the informal teaching situation where children are progressing over a wide area.

It will be seen from the foregoing description of activities around a theme that opportunities for reading, mathematics, recording in writing, for talking purposefully and for increased observation occur all the time in the children's activities. The theme provides the children with a short-term aim which gives their activities purpose and direction. The teacher's aims are long-term and would not make sense to the children even if they were offered explicitly as reasons for learning. The teacher's skill lies in using the children's short-term goals to further her own aims in their education.

For sources of information and book list see p. 15.

2

Containers

The day after the 'Milkman' theme, the teacher decided to develop some of the areas of investigation in a project about 'Containers'.

In discussion she asked the children to tell her the difference between a crate and a milk bottle. This enquiry was extended to include churns and milk floats. Someone suggested that the float was like a big crate on wheels. The difference was one of size and the way the load was conveyed. The class decided to call one type 'Carriers' and the other type (churn, bottle, etc.) 'Containers'. Two labels bearing these names were written out on card and pinned on the wall. A group of children then made drawings of carriers (crate, float, basket, etc.) and these were cut out and pinned under the label 'Carriers'. Another group drew containers and these were pinned up under the appropriate label. Other children made a collection of containers they could find in the classroom. These were put on display on the discovery table and the teacher helped the children write labels for their collection.

On this day both the sand and the water trays were in use. At both trays the teacher suggested the children fill containers and try to put into words what happened. 'What shape is the sand in that box?', 'Will the cardboard box hold water?' were questions she asked.

The teacher wanted to concentrate activities that day on the nature of containers, so she did not ask: 'Will the bottle hold as much sand as it will hold water?', but she was ready with scales and weights if this question did arise. If every opportunity presented by children's activities is followed up at once, there is a danger of discovery being piecemeal and disjointed. One of the teacher's jobs is to see that discovery is sequential and concentrated, and that it can be reinforced and followed up. Ideas about containers, emerging from sand and water activities were linked with other ideas coming from activities at the clay table, the picture-collecting group and the modelling table. Whether a milk bottle holds as much sand as it does water belonged more properly to investigations about liquids and solids and would be followed up along these lines at some other time.

The groups around the sand and water trays were also given wicker baskets and strawberry punnets and asked to fill these with sand and water, and to observe what happened. The children experimented with containers made of other materials. After experiment they made four collections: containers that would hold water and those that would not, containers that would hold sand and those that would not. The teacher used these collections to introduce the idea of overlapping sets. Two large hoops were placed on the floor and into one were put containers that would hold sand, into the other containers that would hold water. The hoops were made to overlap a little and into the overlapping section were placed containers that would hold both sand and water. The children made a drawing of this arrangement. The group who had been collecting containers for the discovery table wanted to arrange their collection in the same way. As some of the containers were large and space was limited the teacher suggested that all three groups work together.

On this day clay was used. The teacher showed the group how to make thumb pots. These were dried and fired in straw (see p. 14 for instructions on firing in straw.)

As containers are three-dimensional, the teacher put aside the painting equipment where expression could be two-dimensional only. At the modelling table children were making trucks and this activity was linked with the group at the book corner where children were finding pictures of vehicles carrying goods. Some of these pictures were in books and these were displayed open on stands below the wall display. The children, with teacher's help, wrote labels to describe what the pictures showed. Other illustrations came from magazines and these were cut out and mounted. The teacher drew a line to represent a road on a long strip of frieze paper and the children pasted pictures of carriers along the 'road'. Another group found pictures of rail trucks. These were pasted along a railway. The children at the modelling table kept coming across to see developments and to get ideas for their models. One child suggested that their models be placed along a road, too. Several tables were pushed together to make a road, and the vehicles were arranged on it. Some children made models of the goods to be carried by their model vehicles.

Later in the day, the teacher took the class to watch traffic along the road by the school and they made a count of vehicles carrying goods. Some children made specialized counts and were able to make a graph when they got back to the classroom: lorries carrying gravel, lorries carrying boxes, lorries carrying metal, petrol tankers, tankers for other liquids. There was great excitement when the children saw both a bulk liquid milk carrier and a milk float.

Back in the classroom, while some children were making the graph, Peter was able to tell the rest about his father's milk float.

In the hall, children mimed carrying heavy and light carriers and containers, filling milk bottles, carrying buckets full of water and so on. They sang 'Little Red Wagon', 'Jack and Jill', 'Polly put the kettle on' and 'There's a hole in my bucket'.

Assessment

During the two days in which they were concerned with the themes: 'The Milkman' and 'Containers' the children had opportunity for discovery and experiment. The themes provided immediate purpose for activities and there was plenty of incidental reading and writing practice. The use of concentrated themes means that the vocabulary specific to the theme is also concentrated and that the same words, embodying ideas, occur in talk, in labels on the wall display, in the books the children used, and were also required in their writing. Meanwhile there was an incentive to read and write and an opportunity to handle words in different ways.

The opportunities for mathematics work were varied. There were opportunities for counting, for sorting and for recording in symbols and in graphs. Most model making requires some mathematical thinking. In every model a child makes there should be further experience in seeing relationships and in shape work. The mathematics specific to the theme: 'Containers' also laid the foundations for further work on capacity. There was a natural opening for introducing Venn diagrams.

For sources of information and book list see p. 15.

In most themes there will be found to be a hard core of activities which provide general practice with a purpose. In addition each theme offers areas of specific learning. These vary with the themes. In both the themes described above the area of specific learning had a bias towards mathematics and some elementary science.

The choice of the next theme may be conditioned by a need to follow up some of this specific learning, or the teacher may decide to change the bias of the next theme so as to give children experience in another area, for example creative art or nature study or linear measure. In this particular class the teacher spent the rest of the week in providing activities in mathematics which reinforced the ideas about capacity. The following week the class embarked on a project from the theme 'Cows and milk'.

3

Cows and Milk

When the teacher produced a picture of a Friesian cow the children were able to tell her that a cow produced milk, that cows were kept on farms. The children who had worked at the book corner the week before were able to tell the rest of the class about some of the processes milk from the farm goes through, on its way to their homes. The teacher suggested that these children show the rest of the class the books which had been most helpful to them. They also described the frieze they had made.

The teacher had several bottles of unpasteurized milk. She showed the children the cream at the top of the bottle and the whiter milk underneath. She shook up one of the bottles and left the cream to settle again. She talked about making butter. The children then went to their group tables and each group was given a jar with a screw top, a jug of *unpasteurized* milk, a spoon and a clean dish. The children shook up the milk in the closed jar and globules of butter began to form. These were spooned out on to the dish. The process continued until no more butter formed. The groups left the rest of the milk to stand, but no cream formed on top. While they were waiting the children ate the butter they had made spread on small cracker biscuits. Some children noticed that it tasted different from the butter they had at home. The teacher suggested they should collect paper wrappings from pats of butter, and she left a tray on the discovery table (labelled 'Wrappings') to receive these when they arrived from home. Some children discovered from reading the butter papers that salt was sometimes added to butter. Later in the week these children made some more butter from creamy milk and added salt to it before tasting. From the butter papers, too, other children discovered that butter comes from New Zealand, Denmark and Eire as well as from Great Britain. For these children the teacher found a map of the world and showed them where these places were.

After the discussion and butter making of the first morning the children again had group activities. The children at the painting corner painted cows in the fields, other children found pictures from magazines, of foods made from milk and butter. A third group found a recipe for cakes made with milk. The teacher wrote out on a large sheet of paper the recipe with ingredients. The children copied this and offered to bring the ingredients from home. Because they could not start making cakes immediately the teacher suggested that they practise weighing because they would need to do so for the cooking operation. The children got out the weighing equipment and the teacher found some general work cards that would direct them to weighing activities. (The teacher had a supply of work cards for each mathematical activity which she used on occasions such as this. The work cards were simple; for example: 'Do three stones weigh as much as three fir-cones?' 'Are fir-cones always exactly the same in weight? What would help you to answer this question?')

At the book corner a group were tidying the books, bringing books on milk and farms to the fore. The children collecting pictures, stuck these into a 'book' made of several pages of brown wrapping paper stapled together. The teacher helped them to write sentences under the pictures. This book was at first hung near the wall display. Later it went on to the bookshelf as a reference book. One of the children from the weighing table copied the recipe for cakes into this book.

Children at the water tray continued the activities with capacity measures that had been started the week before. At the sand tray, children were trying to find which plastic container made the largest sand-pie. The teacher suggested they weigh the sand in the containers before they turned it out. They would then have a comparison by weight as well as height and base width. This investigation was not part of the theme, of course, but the teacher saw that interest was there and felt it was worth following up. One child found that if she drew round the plastic containers she got circles of different sizes. The teacher showed her how to compare these circles for size by folding each cut out circle to get a diameter. Several children started to draw round all the cylindrical objects they could find. The circle thus obtained were arranged in order. Some children drew round the thumbpots made the week before and found that John had made the widest thumbpot. The teacher suggested they record this in writing on a label to be put with the cut-out plans of the pots.

It was not always possible to provide activities for all groups that were directly relevant to the theme. If there was relevance the teacher used it for the sake of concentration. If there was no point of contact then there was still a continuum of discovery which would have relevance to later work. On this occasion the teacher felt that a visit to a farm was needed. Indeed she had started to plan one but knew that it would take a week or two for the plan to mature. In the meantime she was also aware that as soon as the cooking activ'ties started in earnest every child would want to 'have a go'. Hence she structured activities which would include practice in weighing.

The visit to the farm did happen and generated a host of new interests for the children. Themes cannot always be tabulated as providing experiences which fit under neat headings. Nor do all themes provide activities for the full spread of subjects in the curriculum. Where overlap occurs there is a gain in concentration and coherence and the teacher must always be alive to the kind of activities which will contribute to this coherence. But the themes are seen as fitting into a classroom organization which is already rich in activities in which the children can discover and learn, consolidate concepts and practise skills.

No mention has been made in the above description of project activities in an Infant classroom, of the use of stories and poems. The class in question had a half hour story session every day. The teacher used this in a variety of ways. Sometimes she read stories, old favourites and new ones just for the pleasure of sharing a good story with the class or passing on her pleasure in poetry. The story sessions were at the beginning of the afternoon period and were sometimes used to provide a basis for the afternoon's activities in creative craft, free writing, drama and music making.

Sometimes stories and poems were used as 'boosters' to remind children of experiences they had had at some earlier date. For instance, after the visit to the farm a story in the Blackberry Farm series helped to remind the class of their own impressions of the farm they had visited.

Poems used in this way in connection with the themes 'The Milkman', 'Containers' and 'Cows and Milk' are listed on p. 15.

Firing in straw

Obtain a large metal container; a metal wastepaper bin will do. You need real straw. This may be obtained from a stables or wine merchant.

Fire only small and fairly robust objects (small tiles about 1 cm thick or medallions or thumb-pots about 5 cm in diameter).

Put a layer of dry straw in the bottom of the container. Lay some objects on this so that they do not touch one another. Cover with a layer of straw. Place more objects on this. Continue layering until the last layer of straw reaches almost to the top of the container. The objects must be surrounded by straw and must not touch one another. Use plenty of straw but pack it lightly.

Carry the container outside away from buildings and anything inflammable. Set light to the straw by dropping a lighted taper into the container. *Do not lean over the container at any time.*

The straw will burn quickly and fiercely. The heat is sufficient for a biscuit firing. If the clay has not been properly wedged the objects will explode. This is why you must keep well away while the straw is burning. When the fire has died down allow the container to stand for about fifteen minutes. The objects will be hot still but may be removed with metal tongs.

When the objects are quite cool they may be polished with shoe polish. The firing may have scorched some objects but this adds interest to the colouring. Thumb-pots may be burnished with a smooth round stone. They will be found to hold water if there are no holes in them.

This process is only suitable for a first or biscuit firing, but it is quick and easy and the children can observe what happens (from a safe distance of course).

Sources of information

Books

ADAMS, H., *Farms and Farming*, Blackwell (I).

BENDICK, J., *How Much and How Many*, Brockhampton (T/J). and *Measuring*, Z. Watts (T/J).

BOLGER, F. J., *Animal Husbandry* (Rural Studies Series), Blandford (J/T).

EDWARDS, and GIBBON, *Counting and Measuring: Metric*, Burke (J).

GAGG, M. E., *The Farm*, Ladybird (I).

GREE, A., *Keith and Sally on the Farm*, Evans (I/J).

HAVENHAND, I. and J., *The Farmer*, Ladybird (I).

HOLT, E., *The Farmer*, ESA (J).

HUGGETT, F., *Farming* (Junior Reference Books), A. & C. Black (J).

JONES, D., *Cows* (On the Farm), BBC (I/J).

LEWELLEN, J., *Farm Animals* (Junior True Book), Muller (J).

O'KEEFE, J. and RUSH, P., *Weights and Measures*, Methuen (T).

ORAM, S., *Farms and Farmers* (First Library Series), Macdonald (I).

PERRY, G. A., *Farms and Farm Life*, Blandford (J/T).

SWALLOW, S., *Milk* (Starters), Macdonald (I).

WARBURTON, C., *Farming* (Study Book), Bodley Head (J).

Books for model-making

BEETSCHEN, L. (ed.), *Country Treasures*, Mills & Boon (T).

GRATER, M., *One piece of paper*, Mills & Boon (T).

JACKSON, B., *Models from Junk*, Evans (T).

Poems

ANON 'Skip to my Lou', American Traditional.

FLEMING, ELIZABETH, 'The Cow', *All Around You: Poetry Quest*, Blackie.

FROST, ROBERT, 'The Pasture', *Junior Voices I*, Penguin.

MILNE, A. A., 'The King's Breakfast' and 'Summer Afternoon', *When We Were Very Young*, Methuen.

REEVES, JAMES, 'Cows', *Oxford Book of Poetry for Children*, Oxford University Press.

Miscellaneous sources

Wall charts, notes for teachers, booklets, films, filmstrips, leaflets
and booklets for classes of children from:

England and Wales:	National Dairy Centre, John Prince Street, London W1.
Scotland:	Scottish Milk Publicity Council Ltd., 41 Vincent Place, Glasgow C1.
	North of Scotland Milk Marketing Board, Claymore House, 29 Ardconnel Terrace, Inverness.
	Aberdeen and District Dairy Council, Twin Spires, Buckburn, Aberdeen.
Ulster:	Dairy Council for Northern Ireland, 7 Donegall Street West, Belfast.
New Zealand:	New Zealand Dairy Board, St. Olaf House, Tooley Street, London EC1.

Filmstrips

Educational Productions Ltd., 17 Denbigh Street, London SW1:
  Milk, Part I, No. 4898 and *Milk*, Part II, No. 4899 (I/J).

Butter Information Council: *The Story of Butter* (I).

Common Ground Filmstrips: *Milk, Butter and Cheese*, CGB 236 (J).

G.B. Film Library (Filmstrips Dept.) Rank Precision Industries
  Ltd., 1 Aintree Road, Perivale, Greenford, Essex: *The Farm*,
  S65 (I/J).

4

Houses

The project, around this theme, was undertaken by a class of five to six-year-olds. Like the class engaged on the 'Milkman' project there was a wide range of ability. The teacher grouped the children on this occasion according to the roads or streets in which they lived. This was decided in discussion before the project got under way and formed the introduction to the project.

The teacher had made a large outline map of the district in which the children lived. She obtained the details of this map from an Ordnance Survey Map of scale 25 inches to the mile. The names of the roads around the school were clearly written on it.

Each child made a cut-out silhouette of his house in sticky-backed paper. Where children lived in flats or maisonettes the teacher cut out a rectangle to represent a group of these and children cut out windows to show their homes. After much discussion the 'houses' were pinned in place on the map. Discussion ranged about the position of the houses in relation to what could be seen nearby, according to numbers, route to school and so on. If houses had numbers or names the children were encouraged to write these in their 'house' shapes. A group of children was left to stick down the house cut-outs, write in any missing numbers and complete the map by adding trees, pillarboxes, shops, churches and so on according to the evidence supplied by other children. The group working on this was changed from time to time, children living in one street being asked to complete the work on that street.

Another group was painting front views of their houses. Others painted rooms inside their houses. To these paintings were attached sentence labels written by the children with teacher's help. Labels read as follows:

'Mary's house has four big windows at the front.'
'The window downstairs is a bay window.'
'From my flat I can see the school. John'
'My house is built of bricks and metal.'

The children and the teacher had been collecting shoe-boxes for weeks. A group of children now used these to build a wall. They went outside into the playground to look at the way in which bricks were fitted together and copied the arrangement. There were enough boxes to build two walls at right-angles (the corners required much discussion and experiment). The building began to look like a house. A window space was left in the second wall. Even before the walls were finished, some girls were arranging furniture from the Wendy House inside and deciding where a kitchen, living room and bedroom could be made.

At the junk modelling table there were biscuit cartons, wallpaper sample books, large brushes and paper-paste. The children were fashioning rooms inside the biscuit cartons. They chose wallpaper for the walls. Later they made furniture from scraps of wood and also used furniture from the dolls' house. When they had finished they drew their 'rooms' and wrote about how they had been made.

The children at the book corner were looking for illustrations of houses. The teacher made four labels and pinned these on a wallboard. The labels read: 'Flats', 'Maisonettes', 'Houses with gardens', 'Caravans'. Each child was asked to decide which illustration was most like his own house and to write his name underneath the illustration he selected. The pictures were pinned up under the labels. The group doing this involved all the children in the class and the resulting wall display was a picture-graph. It showed that seven children lived in flats, eight in maisonettes, nineteen in houses with gardens and one boy lived in a caravan.

In discussion time, the teacher initiated a discussion about why we need homes. Talk about the need for strong shelter led to a talk about building materials. The teacher suggested that the children collect samples of building materials for the discovery table. One child found a book in the book corner which showed pictures of homes from other periods of history. Another child found one showing homes of people in other lands. The teacher read selected passages from each book and then went on to suggest that although the homes illustrated were built of many different materials and were many different shapes they were all shelters offering protection and privacy.

She then read a story: 'Milly Molly Mandy Keeps House' from Joyce Lankester Brisley's book, *Further doings of M.M.M.* (Harrap, 1964). This led to more discussion about keeping houses clean and tidy. The classroom was not very tidy, so the teacher suggested that the children 'keep house'. Some children swept the floor, others dusted, some washed up crockery, others watered the plants or tidied the shelves. When the classroom was clean and tidy, the children washed their hands and settled down to draw themselves doing one of the jobs. The teacher was able to move from group to group talking to children about their pictures and writing down on scrap paper words and sentences that emerged from these conversations. When the children came to write about their pictures they were able to use these words in their own sentences.

The children's pictures and writings were pinned up on the wall until next day when they were taken down and made into a book for the book corner. Before they went home the teacher asked the children to get their parents to help them write their own addresses on a piece of paper that could be brought to school. The children were also asked to try and make a plan of their own houses 'as though someone had taken the roof off and you could look down into your house or flat'.

Obviously not all children of this age were able to make accurate plans. Some were not able to visualize their houses in this way at all. Parents were able to help others. The teacher's aim was not to obtain accurate plans but to start children thinking along these lines. Later discussion and activities would help with accurate plan making. At this stage children would learn as much from their failures as their successes, and, having tried, would be more receptive to further work about plan-making.

The plans the children brought to school were sketchy, but were used to make a count of rooms. Some children had forgotten or left out rooms like bathrooms and pantries. These omissions were rectified in discussion. The numbers 3 to 7 were put up on the wall and the children pinned their houseplans under the number which corresponded to the number of rooms in their houses.

The teacher then gathered the class around a table where she arranged some dolls' furniture on a board. She then showed the children how she would make a plan of the 'room'. The children working in groups made plans of the positions of furniture in the rooms they had modelled, or furniture in the Wendy House. Others made plans of houses on the floor, using building bricks. Another group made a ground plan of the dolls' house.

In the movement lesson the teacher drew a large groundplan of a house on the floor. With the children's help the rooms were labelled (labels being written on large sheets of card). They played a game in which all the children walked ran or, skipped round the house until the drum stopped beating. They then ran into the 'house' and stood in one of the rooms. The children discovered that the teacher had failed to show openings for doors. This was put right and the game was played several times.

In story time the teacher read from J. M. Barrie's *Peter Pan* how the Lost Boys had built the first Wendy House. After story time the teacher asked the children to supply her with some of the words which had been used about the theme during the two days. The children supplied such words as 'house', 'home', 'room', 'kitchen', 'roof', 'bricks' and so on. Where these words already appeared on wall displays the teacher drew children's attention to the labels in which they appeared. Other words were written by her on blank cards, to be used as flashcards. In the classroom there was a box of flashcards to which children were referred when they wanted spellings for their free writing. The flashcards were used for flashcard practice but were also used in this way and the teacher made sure that any words specific to a theme were available in the flashcard box.

In this class the last session of the afternoon was devoted to reading activities. The non-starters had boxes of apparatus designed to promote reading readiness-jigsaws, directional games, pattern matching cards (see J. M. Hughes, *Aids to Reading*, Evans) Word readers were given the box of flashcards and asked to match up words on the flashcards with those in their reading primers or to make sentences of their own by putting the flashcards together. One small group played games of 'Snap' with especially prepared word cards; another group played a game of 'Pelmanism' with word cards (see p. 25). For children who could read quite well, the teacher had prepared work cards on some of the books in the book corner. On this day the work cards referred to books about houses and homes (see list). Each word card bearing the title of a book had four questions which required the child to read some of the book before giving an answer. Sample questions were: 'Who lives in the kind of house shown on page ten? Draw a picture of him', or 'What furniture did Milly Molly Mandy and Billy Blunt have in their tree house? Design a tree house for yourself and draw it.' The teacher moved from group to group concentrating on getting children to read the words they were handling. She was able to hear four children read from their primers. She was not able to spend much time with the fluent readers but spent five minutes before the children went home in discussing with them, in front of the rest of the class, some of the books they had been reading.

Assessment

After the children had gone home, the teacher recorded the children's progress of the day. She brought the record of children's reading progress up to date by indicating the activities in which they had been employed. She also recorded any conversations she had had with children during the day that had indicated the children were advancing in reading. She made a new record to show how children were progressing towards the idea of ground-plans. The headings for this record, which had the names of all the children in the class down one side, were: 'No idea', 'Tendency to draw front elevations of objects', 'Drawing from on top but confused about levels', 'Drawing from on top but using pictures', 'Drawing from on top and using diagrammatic technique', 'Some idea of proportion', 'Some idea of actual shape of objects represented by plans'. While the children were concerned with plan-making this record was often in use. Later it would be kept in the teacher's file and details entered as individual children showed that they had qualified under one of the headings. This was the teacher's usual procedure. Certain themes produced activities concentrated on a specific area of learning, but the teacher knew that development in this area would not stop when the project around a theme was finished. The children would come to the ideas again in other work. For instance, she knew that having started children on the idea of making ground plans, she would find some of them continuing to do so on their own initiative. She also intended to encourage children making models to prepare plans of these.

Follow-up activities

Several days of warm weather enabled the class to continue the 'Home' theme by investigating the idea of living in a tent. A tent was borrowed from a local scout troop and this was erected in the school field. The teacher was able, also, to arrange a visit to a building site where the children were able to see plans come to life on the ground. These activities provided starting points for discussion in the classroom, and initiated ideas for painting, modelling and free writing. The discovery table with its growing collection of examples of building materials, provided groups with media for sorting and making sets. The materials were eventually classified into natural materials and man-made materials.

On one occasion the teacher set up an investigation into the durability of building materials. The children were sent out to make wax-crayon rubbings of worn parts of the fabric of the school—flaking paintwork, eroded bricks and so on. In the discussion around this, some children suggested that the weather was responsible for the deterioration of the fabric, the heat from the sun, rain and wind being the factors involved. Other children thought that people rubbing or kicking the fabric would cause it to deteriorate. The teacher suggested that the children test these theories.

The children divided into groups. Each group worked around a table on which were placed six building materials: brick, lime-stone, unpainted wood, concrete, slate and glazed tile. One group were given small 'Mouse' files (obtainable at Woolworth's) another group were given piles of newspaper and a hammer, another group worked around the sink with a plastic bowl, and another group had a bucket of dilute vinegar. The last group worked with the teacher because they were to subject their materials to heat from a small paint-stripper blow-lamp. Before beginning the testing the teacher gave each group paper on which to record their results. The group with the files were also given a stop watch. Their instructions were: to rub each sample of building material for ten minutes. The group using the hammer were to place each sample between pads of newspaper and bang it with the hammer. The group at the sink were to subject each sample to a fast jet of water from the tap. (This group wore plastic aprons, for obvious reasons). The next group were to examine the surfaces of their samples using a magnifying glass, then to soak them in weak vinegar for ten minutes, remove the samples to a board to dry out and then re-examine them. The group with the blow-lamp watched as the teacher trained the lamp on each sample. As she did this she talked about the reasons for care when handling fire.

The teacher left her group to record what they had observed and went round to the other groups. The group using the hammer were interested in the different ways in which their samples fractured. Some interesting words came out of discussion here. The brick 'shattered', the limestone 'crumbled', the wood was 'dented' and 'splintered' the concrete 'chipped', the slate 'flaked' and the glazed tile was 'smashed'. The teacher wrote these words on flashcards and the children recorded their observations. The group around the sink had very little to show except a great deal of splashing but became interested in the way the surface of their samples absorbed or resisted water. The teacher showed the group using vinegar that vinegar turned blue litmus paper red. She told them that this was because vinegar was an acid. 'Rain water', she said, 'is also slightly acid.' One child fetched some rain water from a water-butt outside to test this. This group had noticed very little effect on their samples from the soaking in vinegar except that the limestone and the concrete seemed to give off bubbles 'like lemonade'. The teacher told the group that the bubbles were evidence that something—a chemical change—was happening to the limestone and concrete but that it was obvious that the change was very slow. One child noticed that the wood had become very soft and could be squeezed in the hand. The glazed tile and the slate seemed unchanged but the children had observed that the underside of the tile had given off bubbles in vinegar. When, with the teacher's help, all the children had recorded their findings and had cleared away, they settled down to discuss the implications of their tests. The children thought that the 'hammer' test had been rather extreme and that no fabric in a house had to stand up to that kind of treatment in the normal way. All were agreed that untreated wood was vulnerable and the teacher asked them to look out for ways in which wood used in building was protected. The children who had been using water had some interesting things to say about the way water affected surfaces and the teacher used their remarks to show that roofs need special treatment because they are the surfaces which have to keep out the rain. The children were surprised by the way bricks soaked up water. The teacher took them out to show them the damp course. This they saw again on their visit to the building site. The teacher suggested that the class watched what happened when next there was a rainstorm. Did the walls of the house get very wet? Did the rain get through the brickwork to the inside of the house? These and other questions were raised and some had to wait for answers, but the teacher felt she had added a little more to the sum of the children's observations of the world around them. Because this had been an activity shared by the class, any further observations children made would also be shared with the class.

The procedure for testing used on this occasion was one followed by the teacher whenever the material was appropriate. The fairly formal approach helped to lay the basis for careful scientific observation and the activity, with the built-in recording requirement, offered an incentive for writing as well as producing naturally an extended and precise vocabulary.

A project rarely begins and ends neatly. It is not meant to. One of the objectives of project work is to offer for a period of time, a focus of attention around which ideas and vocabulary can accrue, and from which incentives for expressive activities can come. But learning is a continuous process; it is not linear in form but rather like a mesh, the links of which are lines of sequential learning radiating out and touching other learning experiences at many points.

The work provided by the project 'Houses' continued to inform activities in the classroom for as long as the children were there. It became part of the total of their experience. For instance, when the children heard the story of the man sick of a palsy (St Luke 5:18-19) they wanted to know what the roof of the house was made of and why it did not let in the rain.

Pelmanism

This game is based on a game played with playing cards and is not unlike Snap. Indeed the same packs can be used for Pelmanism as for Snap (i.e. two sets of cards with identical faces. About fifteen pairs is enough for a children's game). Place the cards face downwards on a table and move them around to shuffle them. One player picks up a card and turns it over to reveal the face. He does the same with a second card. If the two cards match he removes the pair from the others; this is a 'trick' in his favour. He may then have another turn. If the two cards do not match, the player turns them face downwards in the same position as they were when he turned them up. The other player then turns up two cards. The object of the game is to remember where the card matching the card a player has turned up, is lying.

More children than two can play this game but four is a maximum in class, I think. The game requires a little more skill than snap and makes a useful change.

Cards with words or parts of words on, used in this way, practise recognition of words as shapes on a page. The cards can then be used as flashcards for reading practice.

The advantage of games like this is that they have built-in incentives. They have their own raison d'étre. Children can play games like this without too much supervision. Arguments which may develop between children are learning situations, forcing the children to look more closely at the words in dispute, but a teacher would arbitrate quickly if the argument is noisy or acrimonious.

The words for sets of Snap or Pelmanism cards can come from (a) basic word lists in reading schemes, (b) words around a theme, (c) words which are difficult to spell, (d) words that are often confused, (e) words and distinctive groups of letters in words.

Thus a 'match' in group (a) would be 'Janet'='Janet', in group (b) 'water'='water', in group (c) 'because'='because', in group (d) 'which'='which' and *not* 'witch', and in group (e) 'weigh'='ei' or eigh', 'teacher'='ea' or 'ch'.

Sources of information

Books

ADAMSON, G., *Mister Budge Builds a House*, Brockhampton (J) and *People at Home*, Lutterworth (J).

ADLER, I. and R., *Houses*, Dobson (J/T) and *The Story of a Nail*, Dobson (J).

BLACK, R. I., *Glass*, McGraw Hill (J).

BOWOOD, R., *Story of Houses and Homes*, Ladybird (I/J).

BRANSON, J., *Buildings and Bridges*, Chambers (J).

CARTNER, W. C., *Fun with Architecture*, Kaye & Ward (J/T).

CRABB, E. W., *Living in Old Testament Times*, E. J. Arnold (T/J).

COCHRANE, J., *Glass* and *Timber* (Junior Reference Library), Macdonald (J).

DEMPSEY, M. and WATERS, F., *Metals* (Junior Reference Library), Macdonald (J).

EDWARDS, R. and FLOYD M., *Tower Block*, Burke (J).

EDWARDS, R. and GIBBONS, V., *At Home with the Family* and *Buildings*, and *What Things are Made Of*, Burke (I).

EPSTEIN, S. and B., *Glass*, F. Watts (I/J).

FRY, J. and M., *Architecture for Children*, Allen and Unwin (J).

GIFFIN, F., *Glass*, Muller (T/J).

GREE, A., *Home*, Ward Lock (J).

GREENE, C., *I Want to be a Carpenter* and *I Want to be a Homemaker*, Chambers (I/J).

GORDON-COOK, J., *Look at Glass*, Hamish Hamilton (I/J).

HEILBRONER, J., *This is the House Where Jack Lives*, World's Work (I).

JACOBS, D., *Master Builders of the Middle Ages*, Cassell (J/T).

KING, C., *Building* (People at Work), Blackie (T/J).

LEAVITT, J., *Tools for Building*, Muller (J/T).

LEWIS, M., *Timber* (Many Cargoes), Evans (I).

LUCAS, A. and D., *Building a House*, Methuen (J/T).

MAGUIRE, P., *From Tree-Dwelling to New Towns*, Longman (T).

MOREY, J., *Houses and Homes*, Muller (J/T).

MOSS, P., *Our Own Homes Through the Ages*, Harrap (J/T).

NEWTON, D. and SMITH, D., *Buildings* and *People*, Blackie (J) and *Home Building* (Animal World Series), Longman (J).

RICHARDS, B. T., *Houses* (Men at Work), Longman (J).

ROCKWELL, A., *Glass, Stones and Crown*, Macmillan (T).

SHARP, P., *Crane* (Stand and Stare), Methuen (J).

SHEEHAN, A., *Skyscrapers* (First Library), Macdonald (I).

TAYLOR, B., *Homes*, Brockhampton (J).

THOMPSON, T. A., *Story of Homes*, Blackwell (J).

TRENT, C., *Looking at Buildings*, Dent (J).

TURNBULL, M., *Other People's Homes* (Read and Discover), Hulton (I).

UNSTEAD, R. J., *History of Houses* and *Houses*, Black (J).

WARBURTON, C., *Houses* (Study Books), Bodley Head (J).

WYMER, N., *Timber* (Junior Reference Library), Macdonald (J).

Books about maps

BERG, L., *Finding a Key* (Nippers), Macmillan (I).

BARKER, R., *Maps* (Study Books), Bodley Head (J).

DEMPSEY, M. and SHEEHAN, A., *Shape* (First Library), Macdonald (I).

DEVERSON, HENRY J., *The Map that came to Life*, Oxford University Press (J).

GAGG, J. C., *Maps and Symbols*, Blackwell (I).

HART, T., *Maps and Map-making*, Kaye and Ward (I).

Infant Stories to read and tell

BRISLEY, J., 'Milly-Molly-Mandy finds a nest' from *More of Milly-Molly-Mandy*, 'Milly-Molly-Mandy helps to thatch a roof' and 'Milly-Molly-Mandy camps out' from *Further Doings of Milly-Molly-Mandy*, Harrap.

DUTTON, V. L., *The Little House*, Faber.

GODDEN, R., *Miss Happiness and Miss Flower* and *The Mouse House*, Macmillan.

KEEPING, C., *Charley, Charlotte and the Golden Canary* (a superb picture-story about high-rise flats), Oxford University Press.

Poems

FARJEON, ELEANOR, 'Cottage' *The Tree in the Wood*, Chatto & Windus.

FROST, ROBERT, 'Mending Wall' *Collected Poems of Robert Frost*, Faber.

HERRICK, ROBERT, 'Thanksgiving for his house' *Oxford Book of Verse For Juniors, Book 4*, Oxford University Press.

REEVES, JAMES, 'Animal Homes' *A Puffin Quartet of Poets*, Puffin.

TRADITIONAL, 'This is the house that Jack built' and 'Joshua won the Battle of Jericho' *Junior Voices III*, Penguin.

Filmstrips

'The Home Two Thousand Years Ago', Parts I and II, Religious Films Ltd., 6 Eaton Gate, London SW1.

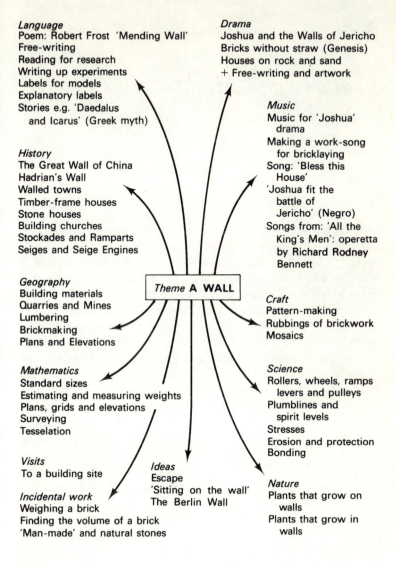

Language
Poem: Robert Frost 'Mending Wall'
Free-writing
Reading for research
Writing up experiments
Labels for models
Explanatory labels
Stories e.g. 'Daedalus
  and Icarus' (Greek myth)

Drama
Joshua and the Walls of Jericho
Bricks without straw (Genesis)
Houses on rock and sand
+ Free-writing and artwork

Music
Music for 'Joshua'
  drama
Making a work-song
  for bricklaying
Song: 'Bless this
  House'
'Joshua fit the
  battle of
  Jericho' (Negro)
Songs from: 'All the
  King's Men': operetta
  by Richard Rodney
  Bennett

History
The Great Wall of China
Hadrian's Wall
Walled towns
Timber-frame houses
Stone houses
Building churches
Stockades and Ramparts
Seiges and Seige Engines

Geography
Building materials
Quarries and Mines
Lumbering
Brickmaking
Plans and Elevations

Theme **A WALL**

Craft
Pattern-making
Rubbings of brickwork
Mosaics

Mathematics
Standard sizes
Estimating and measuring weights
Plans, grids and elevations
Surveying
Tesselation

Science
Rollers, wheels, ramps
  levers and pulleys
Plumblines and
  spirit levels
Stresses
Erosion and protection
Bonding

Visits
To a building site

Incidental work
Weighing a brick
Finding the volume of a brick
'Man-made' and natural stones

Ideas
Escape
'Sitting on the wall'
The Berlin Wall

Nature
Plants that grow on
  walls
Plants that grow in
  walls

Texture table
Building materials (collection)
Man-made and natural
  stones (collection)

Wall display
Pictures and photographs
  of walls and brickwork
All children's models, diagrams,
  paintings and free-writing

5

Feathers and Flight

A Feather

This project was undertaken with a class of post-reception five-year-olds. They were accustomed to working as a class group round the teacher, but in craft work the teacher directed them to activities in small groupings. The ability range in the class was wide. There was a large proportion of non-readers.

Mary brought in a feather she had found. The teacher asked the class to make a collection of feathers. Three boxes were labelled: Stiff feathers, Soft feathers and Half-and-half feathers. The children suggested the labels and the teacher added the words 'stiff', 'soft' and 'feathers' to the cards she had made for flashcard practice (a session of some ten minutes per day was devoted to flashcard work with the whole class).

As feathers for the collection were brought to school they were put in one of these boxes, according to their appearance.

Later the teacher discussed the categories 'Soft', 'Stiff' and 'Half-and-half' and showed the children how feathers were arranged on a bird's wing. The categories were changed to: Flight feathers, Down feathers, Coverts.

After discussion the children were divided into groups. Each group had a box of feathers which they arranged and classified in other ways, e.g. by colour and by size. Numbers of feathers arranged by colour were recorded on block graphs; feathers arranged by size were mounted in order of size.

Later that day, the teacher set up groups for a craft session. The assignments for each group were as follows:

Group 1. Printing with feathers.

Group 2. Cutting feathers out of paper, painting them and using them to make paper birds (see diagram opposite).

Group 3. Collage using fabrics to cover cardboard silhouettes of birds. The teacher was able to reinforce ideas about the way birds' feathers grew when she helped the children to stick feathers, cut out of fabric, on to the bird shapes. The words 'plumage', 'down', 'coverts', 'flight' occurred naturally in these discussions.

Group 4. Painting birds.

When the craft work was cleared away the teacher and children together mounted the results on a wallboard cleared for the purpose. The teacher also displayed some pictures of birds from her collection of pictures. The teacher wrote labels for the pictures and for the children's work. The children suggested the wording for the labels.

The children settled down to draw pictures of themselves working at the various craft activities. The teacher helped them to write sentences about their pictures. This writing was also pinned on the wall display.

Lastly, the children listened to a story: 'The Eagle and the Wren' from *Aesop's Fables*.

The following morning was fine and the children went outside. Working in groups, they were directed to various activities. Some children observed and noted down the number and types of birds that visited the roof of the school. Others made shapes from paper, paper darts, etc. and explored which would 'fly' furthest. This activity was later structured by the teacher so that children stood on a base line and threw their shapes in turn, marking where each shape landed. The children wanted to measure how far their shapes had 'flown' and the teacher suggested that the children measured spans. An argument developed because the spans were not standard and the teacher was able to introduce a standard measure: a 20 centimetre rule. She helped the children with this and showed them how to record the measurements. 'John's dart flew five rulers and five centimetres'.

Another group brought some reference books from the class-room and tried to identify the birds that visited the playground.

MAKING A PAPER BIRD.

Tube of thin card
approximately 6 cm long

15 cm long

Shapes for head, tail
and wings

Wings, head and tail attached thus.

Shapes of feathers.

Feathers attached to card at
base only. Start from wing
tips and tail tips first
so that feathers overlap from
head to tail, and from back
to wing tip.

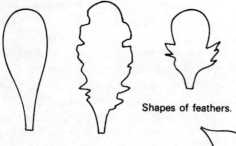

The teacher asked them to watch flight patterns and to notice that some birds flew in an up and down pattern, and others soared or flew in large sweeps. These were identified with the teacher's help. This is not easy, but one of the functions of a teacher is to help children to see. The foundations for this kind of observation began incidentally with observing the flight patterns of the darts. The teacher asked: 'What shape does the dart make in the air? Show me with your arm the shape it makes. Look again.' Later, in dance lesson the children 'flew' up and down or 'soared'.

In the classroom, the teacher put up a graph with columns labelled: Sparrows, Starlings, Blackbirds, Thrushes, Crows. The children could put a tick in the appropriate column whenever one of the species was seen in the playground. The activities of the group making a count of birds, was discussed and the children offered various explanations as to why more birds perched on the roof than rested in the playground. The teacher drew attention to the books, to be found in the library corner, which would help the children to find out more about birds. Lastly the flight patterns of birds, as observed by the children, were discussed and compared with the flight patterns of the paper darts.

As before the children drew pictures of what they had been doing in the playground and the teacher wrote for them (or helped them to write) sentences about their pictures. This time the drawings and pictures were mounted in a scrapbook which was then placed in the Library corner for all children to look at.

The teacher liked to hear the children read from their reading primers as often as possible and this she settled down to do while the class were following the craft activities of the previous afternoon. She was able to hear three children read before the demands of the others drew her away from her desk. She realized, however, that in conversations around the children's drawing/writing activities and in the wealth of written material the wall display was offering, the children were getting reading practice. In the flashcard session the names of the birds seen that morning and words like 'flight', 'plumage', 'perch' were added to the flashcards. The children used the flashcards for spelling reference when they were writing.

The children had a Hall period for music and movement twice a week. The teacher used electronic sounds on record and the children responded with various birdlike movements. The teacher incorporated words like 'glide', 'smoothly', 'jerkily', 'float', 'hop', 'swooping' into her talk about the children's movements to further reinforce the bird theme. The children worked out, in groups, plays about a mother bird teaching her fledglings to fly, and later the teacher read an extract from *The Summer Birds* by Penelope Farmer about some children who learnt to fly*. She could have used the passage from *Peter Pan* when Peter teaches the Darling children to fly.

Assessment

The use of a theme had a 'circular' effect. The children's interest was directed towards a common aim; the vocabulary in discussions, in talk around activities, in the incidental reading material on the walls of the classroom, linked with the theme so that the words were meaningful because they occurred in context. The children's interest was given impetus from time to time through stories, music and dramatic play. Moreover, the children had been given practice in writing with the bonus a theme provides: something to write about and the words to use. The craft work had reinforced the ideas around the theme, the children's observations helped by the teacher had informed the craft. There had been opportunities to sort and classify, to count and to record in graph work; there had been opportunities for the children to select materials with an aim in mind. Lastly, the sharing of ideas and activities had given the class cohesion. The atmosphere of enthusiasm had been self-generating. The children were interested in birds—most children are—they were working together and reluctant sharers were drawn into the general 'busy-ness' of others. The children had something to talk about among themselves and with the teacher.

This project was undertaken in a school which served a suburban estate. This school campus boasted some grass and there were trees around. This need not deter the teacher in a city school from trying a project like this. It is surprising what a wealth of material for nature study is to be found in built-up urban areas. In my experience in city schools in Birmingham I have always found material which can form the basis for a project such as the one outlined above.

*Chapter 8 of T. H. White's *The Sword in the Stone* (Collins) could be used with Junior classes.

Sources of information

Books

ALLEN, G. and DENSLOW, J., *Birds* (The Clue Books), Oxford University Press (I/J).

ALLEN, R., ed. *Book of Birds in Colour*, Hamlyn (J).

ARDLEY, N., *How Birds Behave*, Hamlyn (J/T).

BENSON, S. VERE, ed. *Observer's Book of Birds*, Warne (J/T).

BRANLEY, F., *Birds at Night* (Let's Read and Find Out), Black (I/J).

BURTON, M., *Birds of Britain*, Odhams (J/T).

CAMPBELL, B., *Birds in Colour*, Blandford (J).

CAREY, D., *The Aeroplane* (How it works), Ladybird (J).

CHRISTIE, D., *Birds*, Hamlyn (J).

COCHRANE, J., *Aircraft* (Junior Reference Library), Macdonald (J).

CROOME, A. and WILKINSON, G., *Into the Air*, Brockhampton (I/J).

DAGLISH, E. F., *Name this bird*, Aldine (J).

DARLING, L., *Gull's Way*, Longman (J).

DEMPSEY, M. and SHEEHAN, A., *Air* (First Library), Macdonald (I).

DEMPSEY, M. and WATERS, F. *Birds* (Junior Reference Library), Macdonald (J).

EDWARDS, F., *Birds* (Know About . . .), Young World (J).

FARMER, P., *Summer Birds*, Chatto & Windus (J).

FICHTER, G. S., *Airborne Animals: how they fly*, Pan Books (J).

FISHER, J., *Adventure of the Air*, Rathbone (J).

FITTER, R. S. R., *Your Book of Bird Watching*, Faber (J/T).

GOLDIN, A., *Ducks don't get wet*, Blackie (I).

GREE, A., *Keith and Sally's Bird Book*, Evans (I/J).

HUMPHRIES, L. G., *Man learns to fly*, Blackwell (J).

LEWELLEN, J., *Story of Flight*, Hamlyn (J).

JACKMAN, L., *Exploring the Hedgerow* and *Exploring the Park*, Evans (I/J).

MAKOWSKI, H., *Every Child's Book of Bird-watching*, Burke (J).

PEMBERTON, J. LEIGH, *Garden Birds* and *Pond and River Birds*, Ladybird (I/J).

PLETSCHEN, H., *Ducklings* and *Robin*, Methuen (I).

ROSS, A., *Birds and their lives*, Blackwell (J).

SELSAM, M. E., *Egg to Chick*, World's Work (I/J).

SHOESMITH, K., *Claws, Feathers, Tails* and *Wings*, Burke (I/J).

SOPER, T., *The Bird-table Book*, David and Charles (T).

TAYLOR, R., *Blue-tit, Starling and Sparrow* and *Herring Gull, Mallard, Duck and Swan* and *Robin, Wren and Songthrush* and *Tawny Owl, Jackdaw and Cuckoo*, Methuen (I).

TURNBULL, M., *Birds in the Garden* (Read and Discover), Hulton (J).

VANETTI, G., *The Hen*, Methuen (I).

VEVERS, G., *Birds and their Nests*, Bodley Head (J).

WILDSMITH, B., *Birds*, Oxford University Press (I).

Fiction

CRESSWELL, H., *The Bird Fancier*, Benn (I).

CURTIS, C., *Samantha and the Swan*, Hodder & Stoughton (I).

DE JONG, M., *The Wheel on the School*, Puffin (J).

FARMER, P., *The Seagull*, Hamish Hamilton (I/J).

FARMER, P., *The Summer Birds*, Chatto & Windus (J).

FLACK, M., *Angus and the Ducks*, Bodley Head (I) and *Story about Ping*, Bodley Head (I).

HINES, B., *Kestrel for a Knave* (extracts), Penguin (J).

STOBBS, W., *The Magpie's Nest*, Bodley Head (I).

WHITE, T. H., *The Goshawk* (extracts), Penguin (J).

Poetry

EARP, JAMES, 'The Rook' *Junior Voices II*, Penguin.

FEARN, ELENA, 'Birds', *Poetry Quest* (All Around You), Blackie.

GRAHAME, KENNETH, 'Duck's Ditty' from *The Wind in the Willows*.

KIRKUP, JAMES, 'A Caged Bird in Springtime', *Time for Poetry, Book 2*, Arnold.

KELL, RICHARD, 'Pigeons', *as large as alone*, Macmillan.

MORGAN, EDWIN, 'Starlings in George Square', *Junior Voices IV*, Penguin.

POPA, VESKO, 'Duck', *Junior Voices II*, Penguin.

SUMMERS, HAL, 'Robin', *as large as alone*, Macmillan.
SWENSON, MAY, 'Feel like a Bird', *Junior Voices II*, Penguin.

Filmstrips

'Birds and their Nests' and 'Penguins' from Daily Mail Schools Aids Dept., New Carmelite House, London EC4.
'Our Birds' from Educational Productions Ltd., 17 Denbigh Street, London SW1.
'Life in the Spring' CGB 413, 'Life in the Summer' CGB 415, 'Life in the Autumn' CGB 416 and 'Life in the Winter' CGB 417 from Common Ground Filmstrips, Longman Group Ltd., Harlow, Essex.

Other material

The Royal Society for the Protection of Birds, The Lodge, Sandy, Bedfordshire produces *Birds* magazine, leaflets on bird-watching, feeding birds, etc. Also wallcharts, birdsong recordings and films for hire.

Teacher's Planning

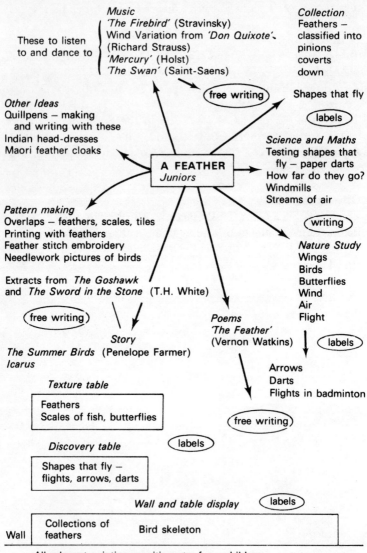

Music
'The Firebird' (Stravinsky)
Wind Variation from *'Don Quixote'*. (Richard Strauss)
'Mercury' (Holst)
'The Swan' (Saint-Saens)

These to listen to and dance to

Collection
Feathers —
classified into
pinions
coverts
down

free writing

Shapes that fly

labels

Other Ideas
Quillpens — making and writing with these
Indian head-dresses
Maori feather cloaks

A FEATHER
Juniors

Science and Maths
Testing shapes that fly — paper darts
How far do they go?
Windmills
Streams of air

writing

Pattern making
Overlaps — feathers, scales, tiles
Printing with feathers
Feather stitch embroidery
Needlework pictures of birds

Nature Study
Wings
Birds
Butterflies
Wind
Air
Flight

Extracts from *The Goshawk* and *The Sword in the Stone* (T.H. White)

free writing

Story
The Summer Birds (Penelope Farmer)
Icarus

labels

Poems
'The Feather'
(Vernon Watkins)

Arrows
Darts
Flights in badminton

Texture table

Feathers
Scales of fish, butterflies

free writing

Discovery table

labels

Shapes that fly —
flights, arrows, darts

Wall and table display

labels

Wall	Collections of feathers	Bird skeleton

All relevant paintings, writing etc. from children
Results of testing. Illustrations of 'Summer Birds'

Labels written with quill pen

6

A Christmas Pudding

There were three weeks to go before the end of the Autumn term. The children were already talking about Christmas. The teacher wanted a theme that would exploit their interest but still maintain a serious atmosphere of learning in the class which was a vertically grouped one of children from five to seven years.

She brought in a Christmas pudding and invited children to bring ingredients for the class to make its own. The teacher wrote out a list of ingredients, with measures, and a simple recipe, on a large sheet of art paper and pinned it to the wall.

She also wrote a series of labels and placed them on several tables so that when the ingredients began to come in children could place them against the appropriate labels on the tables.

Knowing that in making the pudding, children would need to weigh ingredients, the teacher placed several types of weighing machines and a set of weights very prominently on the discovery table and directed children to their use by a series of instructions both oral and written. Older children were also given assignment cards to direct them to weighing activities.

Sample Instructions
Weigh a stone. Weigh a brick. Weigh two bricks. Weigh a full milk bottle. Weigh an empty milk bottle. Weigh a book.

Assignment Cards
Find something which weighs 10 grammes.
Find something which weighs 5 grammes.

Find two things which when weighed together are exactly 10 grammes.

A group of children at the pre-reading stage played a game called 'Ingredients'. The teacher made some large flashcards bearing the names of all the ingredients needed to make the pudding and some cards bearing other words. (The words on the cards were repeated so that there were 24 cards in all.) The cards were then shuffled face downwards on the table and each child picked a card in turn until all the cards were dealt (two, three, four or six children can play with 24 cards but six is really too many). A large mixing bowl like that which would be used to mix the Christmas pudding was placed in front of the children, who looked at their cards in turn and decided whether the legend indicated an ingredient for the pudding or not. They could check the flashcard against the list of ingredients on the wall. Each child used one card in turn. The winner was the one who had the least cards left. (This game can be varied if, after having a turn, each child passes a card face downwards to the next child.)

Children painted what the Christmas pudding would look like, and a few of the older children discovered where the ingredients came from and how they were processed. One group tried turning grapes into sultanas by drying them in an oven, another group ground some grains of wheat between two large pebbles and made flour. They wrote about what they did and used their writing as extended labels when the results were displayed on a table. Two children made a book about a Christmas pudding. The recipe was carefully copied on to the front page and, using information brought to them by other children, the two scribes wrote about the ingredients. They left some pages so that they could record the making of the class Christmas pudding.

The teacher told the story of the 'Gingerbread Man' substituting a Christmas pudding for the gingerbread man. She also read them Dickens's description of the Cratchits' Christmas pudding.

The day arrived when the pudding was to be made. All the tables were covered with clean cloths and the children all wore aprons and washed their hands. The tables were labelled 'Ingredients', 'Weighing', 'Dry mixing', 'Wet mixing', 'Creaming', and the children were assigned to one or other of these tables where appropriate utensils were found. The Ingredients table supplied the ingredients which were weighed by the children at the weighing table, and then passed to either the dry mixing, wet mixing or creaming group. When all the ingredients were mixed together, each child stirred and, naturally, made a wish. Bowls were greased, the pudding mixture doled out. The puddings, for several were made, were steamed by a friendly parent, and a cook in the school canteen was persuaded to heat them so that the children could eat their puddings one lunch time.

The whole class recorded the experience in painting, drawing, drawing and writing and in clay modelling, and the results of their efforts were put together for a display in the corridor where their experiences could be shared with other classes.

Assessment

As this was the first venture of this class into activities around cooking, part of the activities was teacher-directed. The teacher provided the recipe and showed children how to proceed. Cooking became part of the repertoire of this class and the children learned to follow instructions given in recipes to make other topical dishes: Welsh Cakes (St David's Day), Potato cakes (St Patrick's Day), Scones (St Andrew's Day), Hot Cross Buns, a birthday cake and gingerbread.

Cooking could be one activityi n themes around Milk (see p. 12). Flour, Eggs, Parties, Making moulds (Liquids into solids or commodities that are shaped in moulds, e.g. cast iron), Preserving (drying and bottling apples are fairly straightforward operations).

Cooking activities involve counting, classifying, tactile discovery, observation on the behaviour of liquids and solids (powders and fats, raising agents), reading activities and the following of written instructions (sequential activities).

The ability to follow a series of steps in instructions is a valuable part of scientific training. When children have been taken through the procedure with a teacher's help, they may be able to follow written instructions for themselves. The teacher may provide 'recipes' for such procedures as mixing paste or paint, or written instructions for clearing up after painting, like this:

Clearing up after painting
Wash your brushes in the water jar and lay them on newspaper.
Carry water to sink (or bowl) and tip away water. Turn the jar
upside down on drainer.
Put your painting to dry on the back of your chair or on the
clothes horse.
Put your paint tray in the cupboard.
Wipe your palette with your painting rag and put the palette on
the shelf.
Put your brushes into the bucket of clean water provided.
Fold the dirty newspaper and place it near the wastepaper bin.
Wash your hands.
Write a label for your painting at the writing table.

Sources of information

Books

BATES, M., *Talking about Puddings*, Pergamon (J/T).
BROOMFIELD, R., *The Twelve Days of Christmas*, Bodley Head (I).
COONEY, B., *Christmas*, Oliver & Boyd (J/T).
COOPER, E., *All Things Nice*, Lutterworth Press (I/J).
GOAMAN, M., *Food Through the Ages*, Ladybird (I/J).
HAINES, G. H., *Food* (How We Find Out), J. Baker (J).
HARRISON, M., *Food*, ESA (J).
HOARE, R. H., *St. Nicholas* (Our Saints), Longman (I).
KLAGSBRUN, F., *Spices*, F. Watts (I/J).
LEWIS, M., *Grain* and *Sugar* (Many Cargoes), Evans (I).
MOSS, P., *Meals Through the Ages*, Harrap (J/T).
NORTHFIELD, E., *Food* (Study Books), Bodley Head (J).
O'CONNOR, M., *First Steps in the Kitchen*, Faber (J).
PEARSON, N. F., *Christmas Customs*, Ladybird (J).
PETERSHAM, J., *The Story Book of Sugar* and *The Story Book of Wheat*,
    Wells Gardner (I/J).
RUSSELL, S. P., *About Fruit* (Junior Look, Read Learn), Muller (J).
SCHEIB, I., *Food* (First Book), F. Watts (I/J).
SHANNON, T., *About Food and Where it Comes From*, Muller (J).
SWALLOW, S., *Milk* and *Eggs* (Starters), Macdonald (I).

WAKELAM, T., *Your Reference Book of Nuts* and *Your Reference Book of Sugar*, Cambridge University Press (J).

WORTHY, W., *A Bowl of Fruit* (All About . . .), Longman (J).

Miscellaneous Sources

Various pamphlets and teacher's study kit about sugar from British Sugar Bureau, 140 Park Lane, London W1.

Project notes No. 5 'Mediterranean harvest' from Cadbury Schweppes, Bourneville, England.

Pamphlets about wheat with samples (for teachers) from Flour Advisory Bureau, 21 Arlington Street, London SW1.

'The Story of a Bag of Flour' for children from McDougalls Ltd., Wheatsheaf Mills, London E14. This is free but limited to 50 copies per school.

7

A Stone

Johnny brought in a stone which he had found on the way to school. Johnny and some friends cleared the discovery table and Johnny's stone was placed upon it. The teacher wrote a label with Johnny's help; 'Johnny's stone is hard and smooth'.

A group of children were sent out into the playground to find hard and smooth stones, hard and rough stones, crumbly stones. When these were brought back they joined Johnny's stone on the discovery table, duly labelled.

Meanwhile another group of children were looking through old magazines for pictures to cut out. They found some pictures of mountains, stones in a river, a pebbly beach and a road. These were mounted on the wall. The teacher wrote some labels and left three children to drawing-pin the labels where they matched pictures. Another group used similar pictures to stick into a scrap-book. (The teacher always had available a few spare scrap-books made up from pastel paper.)

The teacher took the whole class out to the road, where they looked at the road surface. Some stones could be seen embedded in the tar, others were loose and had collected in the gutters. The teacher asked the class why stones were used to cover road and path surfaces, and why they needed to be bonded in some way. On the way back the children looked at the gravel path, a paved path, and the school playground.

A group of children painted paths; gravel paths and the patterns of paved paths. Mary painted herself walking down a pebbly beach to paddle. The paintings went up on the wall. Everyone looked at them and decided what teacher should write about them.

Another group used sand and pebbles to make a collage. They looked at the sand through a magnifying glass and saw that it was composed of tiny pebbles. The teacher put a magnifying glass on the discovery table. The collages were mounted on the wall and the teacher helped children to label their work.

Later that afternoon the teacher told the children a story (made up by herself) of the adventures of a rough stone in a rushing river. Afterwards she read them the poem: 'Pebbles' by Edith King from *All Around You*, Poetry Quest Series.

The following day the class, a vertically grouped one, with children aged from five plus to seven, used stones in all their mathematics activities. The younger children sorted stones according to their own criteria by colour and shape. Later the teacher suggested they sort the stones by texture. Some of the younger children used stones in weighing (they were not yet using standard weights) and recorded their findings, e.g. three stones weigh as much as ten shells. The older children also classified stones. Each stone was weighed in grammes and the weight recorded on a label and put by the appropriate stone. The stones were then arranged in order of weight. The teacher introduced a spring balance for some of the seven-year-olds to use. The children then drew pictures of what they had been doing and wrote about the pictures.

Later that day the children discovered how quickly different rocks eroded. The teacher set up 'testing' procedures (see p. 23). After the discussion which followed this session, the samples were arranged on the discovery table and the children suggested the wording of accompanying labels. The teacher then shook up a tablespoonful of gravel in a jam-jar of water and left the mixture to settle. After playtime the children could see levels of sedimentation had appeared at the bottom of the jar. They compared the appearance of these with the texture of some of the stones and came to the conclusion that stones are made up of even smaller particles. The next day the teacher made up a small quantity of concrete and moulded it into a brick. She asked the children to

45

try and identify objects made of concrete as they walked home from school.

The teacher found an opportunity to read some of 'Mending Wall' by Robert Frost, and asked the children to notice where walls were made. She showed them pictures of dry-stone walling but it was some months before children actually saw some.

In Hall periods the children acted that they were walking on sharp pebbles, smooth pebbles, on gravel and on tarmac. They mimed building a wall and laying a road surface. They then sang and acted 'Joshua and the Walls of Jericho' published in *Junior Voices*, III.

This was a theme arising from something a child had brought to school. The theme 'Stones' can be followed by one on precious stones which can lead to work on prisms, crystals and jewellery, and has links with several traditional stories. One class were fortunate in obtaining some samples of uncut and cut gemstones on loan from a local museum.

Other themes arising from what children bring in are: leaves (opportunities for printing, sorting and setting, finding areas, pattern-making, appliqué needlework as well as links with several stories and a wealth of poetry), Seeds, Fur, Feathers (see p. 30), A toy vehicle, Tadpoles, A nest, A plant, Shells, A fish, A foreign coin or stamp, A pet.

Sources of information

Books

ADLER, I., and ADLER, R., *The Earth's Crust*, Dobson (J/T).

ALLWARD, M., *The Earth*, Collins (J).

BARKER, R. S., *The Land* (Study Books), Bodley Head (J).

BEETSCHEN, L., *Holiday Treasures*, Mills & Boon, (I/J).

BETHERS, R., *What Happens Underground?*, Macmillan (I/J).

BLACKWOOD, P., *Rocks and Minerals*, Transworld (J).

CARTNER, W., *Fun with Geology* and *Fun with Palaeontology*, Kaye & Ward (J/T).

CROSBY, P., *Rock Collecting*, Muller (T/J).

ELLIS, C., *Pebble on the Beach*, Faber (T).

EVANS, I. O., *The Observer's Book of Geology*, Warne (T/J).

GANS, R., *The Wonder of Stones*, A. and C. Black (I).

KIRKALDY, J. F., *Fossils in Colour*, Blandford (J).

KNIGHT, D. C., *The Earth*, F. Watts (J).

LEVINE, J. and PINE, T. S., *Rocks all around* (All Around . . .), Blackie, (J/T).

MCKAY, H., *Half-hours with Geology*, Oxford University Press (J/T).

MATTHEWS, W. H., *Wonders of Fossils*, World's Work (J/T).

MILBURN, D., *First Book of Geology*, Blackwell (J).

MUNARI, B., *Search for a Stone*, A. and C. Black (I).

MURRAY, I., *Seashore*, A. and C. Black (I).

PODENDORF, I., *Rocks and Minerals*, Muller (J/T).

SMITHERS, R., *Your Book of the Earth*, Faber (J/T).

SWINTON, W. E., *The Earth Tells its Story*, Bodley Head (T/J).

TRENT, C., *Exploring Rocks*, Dent (J).

WATERS, F., *Rocks and Minerals* (Junior Reference Library), Macdonald (J)

WHITE, A., *Story of our Rocks and Minerals*, Ladybird (J).

WRIGLEY, D., *Sand*, Lutterworth, (J).

WYCKOFF, J., *Secrets of the Earth* and *Rocks and Minerals*, Hamlyn (J).

Poems

CUMMINGS, E. E., 'maggie and milly and molly and may' from *as large as alone*, Macmillan.

HUBBELL, PATRICIA, 'Gravel Paths', *Junior Voices II*, Penguin.

KING, EDITH, 'Pebbles', *Poetry Quest* (All Around You), Blackie.

REEVES, JAMES, 'The Sea', from *as large as alone*, Macmillan.

8

Hands

'What a lot of things we can do with our hands. We can touch, and stroke, and clap, and play the piano, hold pencils, catch balls, and make shadow animals.' Thus said a teacher to a class of post-reception five-year-olds. She was introducing the theme 'Hands' as part of a series of themes on 'Myself'. She had come in to the classroom, before the children and had arranged a 'Touch' table with a selection of things to feel and touch. She had also put some irregular shaped articles in a black draw-string bag and left this on the 'Touch' table with a question card saying: 'Guess by feeling, what things are in this bag.' During the day she drew children's attention to the table and to the guessing bag.

The teacher had also put away the paint brushes, and mixed paint rather more thickly than usual for today the children were going to try finger-painting.

But first the children looked at their hands. They counted their fingers, counted the joints on each finger and looked at the patterns on the skin of the finger-tips. The teacher had an ink pad, normally used with a rubber stamp. She showed the children how to make fingerprints and then left a group to do so. Using illustrations from the book *Your Skin and Mine* edited by Franklyn Branley (A. and C. Black) the group were able to decide on individual patterns of fingerprints.

Another group were asked, 'What can you measure with your hands?' Some children used their fingers spread wide, some children used the length of their hands from wrist to fingertip. The teacher suggested that it might be easier if they drew round their hands and made a pattern-shape which they could use as a measure. Some children cut out several shapes and used them to show how many spans high the blackboard was. The teacher told them about measuring the height of horses in 'hands'.

Another group went to the book corner where the teacher had placed prominently some books about the body. One boy found a picture of animal 'hands'. They saw that lizards and monkeys have five fingers on each 'hand'. They visited a pet rabbit in another classroom to look at its paws. The headteacher's dog seemed to have four claws on each paw and a little one like a thumb up the leg. The teacher made a label 'Hands, paws and claws', and drawing-pinned it to a wallboard. The children made drawings of some animal claws and paws and with the teacher's help labelled them with the name of each animal. These were put up on display. Meanwhile some other children at the book corner were looking through piles of illustrations. At teacher's suggestion some were searching for illustrations of people using their hands, others for illustrations of animals. When these pictures were found the children trimmed them and pinned them on the display board. Later they took them down and stuck them into a scrap book which the teacher helped them to label to make a reading book for the library. They used one girl's finger-painting to decorate the cover.

Later in the day the teacher showed them some finger plays and they sang a song about 'Hands'. They also clapped various rhythms.

Using the cut-outs of hands the children counted. 'How many fingers on three hands?' asked the teacher. 'How many fingers on five hands?'

In the Hall the activities were all to do with throwing and catching. Some children tried to stand or walk on their hands. They finished with a wheelbarrow race.

Just before everybody went home the class looked at the wall display and the teacher read some of the labels to the children, and showed them the pictures in the scrapbook.

Assessment

The elements in this project were:

1. Mathematical.
   Pattern-making—introduction to counting in five and tens.
   Measuring—this could be developed further at another time into exploring the need for standard units of measurement.
2. Texture, leading to printing, and also language about *feel* of things.
3. Painting, drawing and writing.
4. Reading activities—labels—making a book—using books for reference.

Similar themes include feet, heads, teeth, mouths, noses, ears, hair. The hygiene element in these investigations should not be overlooked.

Sources of information

Books

ALLEN, G., *Bones* and *Claws* (Clue Books), Oxford University Press (I/J).

'ALIKI', *My Five Senses*, Blackie (I).

BORTEN, H., *Do You Move As I Do?*, Abelard Schumann (J).

BRANLEY, F., *Big Tracks and Little Tracks*, Blackie (I).

HUMPHRYS, L. G., *Your Body At Work*, Blackwell (I/J).

MASON, G., *Animal Tools* and *Animal Tracks*, Dent (J/T).

SHEEHAN, A., *Size* (First Library), Macdonald (I).

SHOESMITH, K. A., *Do You Know About Claws?*, Burke (I).

JONES, J., *Glove Puppetry*, Brockhampton (J/T).

Poems

FARJEON, ELEANOR, 'Tailor', *Poetry Quest* (All Around You), Blackie.

HUGHES, TED, 'Grandma', *Poetry Quest* (Through the Five Senses), Blackie.

ROBERTS, C. G. D., 'Old Morgan', *Poetry Quest* (Through the Five Senses), Blackie.

ROETHKE, THEODORE, 'Transplanting' (first verse), *Junior Voices IV*, Penguin.

SWENSON, MAY, 'Cat and the Weather' and 'Feel Like A bird', *Junior Voices II*, Penguin.

THORLEY, WILFRID, 'Song for a Ball Game' *Poetry Quest* (All Around You), Blackie.

WALKER, TED, 'Father's Gloves' *Junior Voices IV*, Penguin.

WALSH, JOHN, 'Blind Boy on the Shore', *Poetry Quest* (It Could Happen To You), Blackie.

9

Time

The class was a first-year Junior class with a wide range of ability in reading and free writing. The children had come from several Infant schools. The teacher needed to assess the attainment of the children, and also to weld them into a class unit. She felt that her job in the first term was to consolidate the reading, free writing and mathematical experiences of the children gained in the Infant schools. She knew that the children would feel insecure at first in a changed situation and would need time to grow accustomed to working in new groups, but she wished also to continue the process which is one of the aims of primary education, that of lessening the children's dependence on the teacher as a source of knowledge and inspiration and of developing the children's initiative. This process is gradual and may not be achieved until the fourth year of Junior school.

The teacher chose the theme: 'Time'. She thought this theme would offer opportunities for investigation and experiment. The children would not have to go too far afield for their observations. There would be an emphasis on direct experience rather than book-based experience. There would also be emphasis on ways of recording research and observation.

She intended to introduce simple work cards to direct children to single assignments. The wording on the work cards would be brief enough to be *read to* the non-reader, but the use of work cards would offer incentives perhaps, for children beginning to read. The work cards would outline the scope of the project around the 'Time' theme, and introduce some of the vocabulary in written form. Because of the fairly narrow area of investigation in which she intended to start, the work cards would overlap in the assignments they set children and would help to form children into fairly flexible groups. She wanted to avoid arbitrary groupings, preferring children to work together where they could co-operate around similar ideas and share discovery and information.

The classroom was organized so that children had work spaces (several flat-topped desks pushed together) for practical work and for recording. In the book corner books on the theme were displayed prominently. The discovery table contained an old clock (the hands could be moved), the mechanism and pendulum of a cuckoo-clock, an egg-timer, a metronome and a stop-watch. The teacher cleared space for a wall display to tell the 'story' of the project as it progressed.

Other material collected by the teacher included a quantity of dry sand (silver sand is obtainable from gardeners' suppliers or dry salters) scoops, funnels and plastic bottles. A rubber-stamp to print clock faces was also provided. The teacher laid out squared paper of various graduations. She arranged for a newspaper to be brought in daily and laid out copies of the current *Radio Times* and some bus and train timetables.

The wall display was begun with four pictures of children getting up in the morning, coming to school, having an evening meal, and going to bed. Under each picture was a question: What time do you get up? What time do you start out for school? What time do you have your evening meal? What time do you usually go to bed?

One evening, just before the class went home the teacher suggested that they discover the answers to some or all of these questions. The children's first job the following day was to print clock faces and show times at which these things happened for them. They wrote their names on the papers and mounted them under the appropriate pictures. Children who had forgotten to get this information filled in their clock faces later.

The teacher then gave out work cards. Cards were given to pairs of children. Inevitably larger groups formed around books, at work tables around the wall display and so on. Children could move about the classroom freely. There was no embargo on talking and children were constantly aware of what others were doing. The teacher liaised between groups and saw that if the work of one group could help another the two were brought together.

These work cards were designed to provide starting points *only* for children's investigations, and starting points for teaching. They were not meant to be self-correcting or to occupy the children on their own for long periods of time. Using work cards like these means that children can make a beginning, that is collect equipment, reference books, etc., and start thinking about the problem. The teacher moves from group to group furthering the work by questions, and by offering information the children may not be able to find out for themselves.

The work cards were as follows:

A. Make a timetable of your day, beginning when you get up. Show times like this: 8.30 a.m., and also in writing, like this: 'I got up at half-past seven in the morning.'

B. Make a list of your favourite TV programmes and draw clocks to show at what times they start.

C. Make a timetable to show what happens at school on Mondays. Draw clocks and record in writing like this: 'We come into school at five minutes to nine in the morning.'

D. Use information from the wall display to show the times at which children in the class go to bed. Make a graph.

E. Make a clock face with movable hands and use it to teach someone to tell the time.

F. Why do clock faces have figures and marks around their faces? Design a twenty-four-hour clock face.

G. How many times does the hour hand go round the clock face in 12 hours? Draw a clock face and colour in the part (segment) between 3 o'clock and 6 o'clock. How much of the clock face have you coloured? Answer in writing.

H. Find a way of recording one minute of time. How many times does your pulse beat in one minute? Record in writing.

I. Make a timer to show when five minutes of time have passed.

J. Make a timer to show when one minute of time has passed. Use it to see how many names of children you can write down in one minute.

K. Use a stop-watch to record the time taken by your partner to run all round the perimeter of the playground. Time other children in the class. Who ran fastest?

L. Make a model of a Roman water-timer (clepsydra). How long a passage of time does your model measure?

M. Make a pendulum with a string as long as a metre ruler. How many full swings does it make in one minute?

N. Make a pendulum with a string of 20 centimetres. How many full swings does it make in one minute? Compare your results with the findings of children using card M.

O. Set up and keep a graph showing times of sunrise over one week. On the same grid show times of sunset. Will this be a block graph or a line graph?

P. Make a graph to show lighting-up times over one week. By how many minutes does this vary each day? Compare your graph with the one showing times of sunset.
(Lighting-up times are shown in 'current' time but sunrise and sunset are often given in newspapers as GMT. This could be an interesting discussion point.)

Q. Do you go to bed before or after sunset this month? Do you get up before or after sunrise this month? By how many minutes does your rising and bedtime differ from sunrise and sunset each day this week? Show this difference mathematically.

R. Find out how passage of time is indicated aboard ship. Divide the school day into 'watches'. What will you be doing in the forenoon watch? Record in writing.
[The teacher possessed a *Seaman's Manual* (HMSO) which gave this information. Otherwise this may have to be an optional assignment if information is not readily available.]

S. The Ancient Egyptians used the sun as a timekeeper. Could you use it? Make a sun-clock. Draw pictures of other sun-clocks and sun-dials.

T. Make a time chart to show when members of your family were born. Begin like this: 1895 Grandmother born.

U. Find out when the school was built. Is it older or younger than you? Show the difference in years mathematically.

Having given out the work cards, the teacher said that she would be 'deaf, dumb and blind for ten minutes', to give the children a chance to puzzle out the wording on the cards by helping one another, and time to discuss the cards with their partners without reference to her. The class was noisy but the talk was purposeful.

For the rest of the period of forty-five minutes the teacher helped the children to make a start, indicating books that might help, discussing the setting up of grids for graphs, liaising between groups.

By the time she reached the children making pendulums they had already found a picture of one in *The Study Book of Time and Clocks*, and they were measuring out some string. The teacher checked the length of the strings pointed out that some string would be needed to tie around the stone used as a pendulum bob, if indeed that was what they were going to use. She came back to this group later, when the pendulums had been successfully made, and suggested that a blob of thick paint at the bottom of the pendulum bob would make lines as the pendulum swung over a sheet of white paper placed on the floor. In this way the lines of swing would be easier to count and the record of the number of swings would be already made. This activity attracted several other children in the class. Attractive patterns were being produced. The teacher suggested that other children might make pendulum patterns when they had finished their own assignments.

She showed the group about to go into the playground, how to use a stop-watch. She went out later to find that they had not taken pencils and paper with them. Memories being unreliable, records should be made at every stage. The children appointed a scribe.

At the end of the session the children drawing-pinned any recorded evidence of their work however unfinished under the wall display. In the five minutes before playtime the teacher discussed some of the problems that had arisen and made suggestions for further group work.

After playtime the teacher showed the class how to make a candle timer. Two candles of equal dimensions were marked off (by sticking dressmakers' pins into the wax) in equal graduations of 2 centimetres between pins. The children were asked to invent a name for the unit of time represented by these sections. They suggested minutes and hours, but these were rejected as being names already invented for units of time. They invented the name 'CAN' for the unit. The teacher said they would have some flashcard practice for the length of a CAN. One candle was lit and the practice began.

The teacher added the words Time, Minute, Second, Hour, Day, Month, Year, Passage, Difference, Sunset, Sunrise, Lighting-up time, Darkness, Daylight, and Sunlight to the flashcard box, writing these in front of the children and asking some children to match individual flashcards with words on labels on the walls. Other words from the basic word list of the reading system in use in the class, were already written on flashcards. Each flashcard 30 cm by 5 cm had a strip of coarse sandpaper stuck to the back of it. A flannelgraph (a strip of flannel or felt 50 cm by 50 cm) was pinned to the blackboard. The flashcards with sandpaper backing adhered to this. Pictures to illustrate some of the words had been cut out and backed in the same way. Sometimes flashcard practice consisted in the teacher holding up a card which the class 'read' in chorus, but on this occasion the teacher suggested that the children offer sentences using the new words to do with time. Sentences like: 'John can tell the time', 'Janet goes to bed in daylight' were offered and these were assembled on the flannelgraph.

When the candle had burned down to the first pin-marker, the teacher stopped the flashcard work and suggested that the children draw pictures of what they had been doing before playtime. They could then write about their pictures with words from the flashcard box to help them. The pictures and writing were done on loose paper so that they could act as labels for the display. The teacher said that the class would have two 'CANS' of time to complete their pictures and writing.

As soon as the children settled down to draw the teacher began to move among them discussing what they would write about the pictures. As children completed their writing she heard them read what they had written. Spellings came not only from the flashcards but from words on the wall display, from the children's reading primers, and from the work cards.

After two 'CANS' had elapsed the teacher left some children to decorate their work with writing patterns, finish their writing or elaborate their pictures while she heard others read from their reading primers.

In the afternoon the teacher introduced a music session by getting children to feel their pulses. She then asked six children to beat out the pulse rhythm on drums or tambours while the rest of the class recited words like 'pendulums, second, timetable, clock'. A group reciting the word 'pendulum' played the rhythm of the word on triangles, those reciting 'second' on tambourines, those reciting 'timetable' on resi-resis. The children who had been reciting 'clock' were asked to choose an instrument most suggestive of the word. After some trials they selected Chinese blocks. The class then played their rhythms separately, in fugue and altogether. After a little practice they were able to fit the differing rhythms together quite well. The drums and tambours maintained a steady pulse beat. The class then sang 'Hickory, dickory dock' with a percussion piece at the beginning and the end of the song. The teacher taught them to sing 'The Grandfather Clock'.

On another occasion in the school hall the children working in groups of three, mimed the parts of a clock: wheels, pallets and hands. The teacher gave them time to practise moving smoothly together and then divided the class into halves. One half played the percussion piece they had devised in the music session, the other half mimed the workings of clocks. The two groups changed about and tried again. Back in the classroom the teacher read 'The Grandfather Clock', a poem by Hugh Chesterman from *It Could Happen to You*.

The project around the theme 'Time' lasted two weeks. During that period the teacher gave a talk to the class on the history of time-keeping and emphasized the distinction between clocks and other instruments which merely recorded passage of time. The two weeks were long enough to allow the sun-clock to be completed and discussed, to allow more recording on the graphs by another group of children. Assignments were considered to be completed when each child had recorded the work in writing and mathematically in a 'sum', diagram or graph. All the work was mounted on the wall display. The work cards were mounted near the children's recording. Children who finished one assignment could choose another. Not every child could do every work card but the teacher devoted some time each day to discussing with the class what had been done or she asked the children themselves to tell others what they had been doing.

The teacher gave the class a lesson on drawing grids for graphs. This was to remind them of what they had learned before about graphs, and to teach some new vocabulary: 'grids' and 'co-ordinates'. The teacher used the information from the wall display as material for the graphs. The information about bedtimes, etc. was best recorded as a block graph, but the teacher showed that line graphs were better for other kinds of information that varied uniformly from day to day, like lighting-up times. She pointed out what could be deduced from a block graph and from a line graph and in the following week one mathematics session was devoted to work cards asking children to deduce information from the graphs on the wall display.

In spare minutes the children taught each other to tell the time and the teacher kept records of their progress in learning to tell time. The teacher constantly drew attention to clock time by saying at appropriate moments: 'It is now x o'clock', and adjusting the hands of the model clock to show the time. She used the candle clock too to record passage of time.

She gave one creative craft session so that all the children could make pendulum patterns.

This theme and project was followed by one on 'Time charts'. The children were encouraged to work backwards from their own birth dates to the dates of birth of their parents and grandparents, and to find out something of what life was like around these dates. The historical researches were confined to clothes, vehicles, and kitchens. Later, other investigations were made into 'Seasons', 'Time round the world', 'Ship's time', 'Timetables'. It will be seen that some of these ideas had already been introduced in the project described but that work had concentrated on some areas to the partial neglect of others.

In a school where there is an overall Mathematics scheme, a theme like the one described could be slotted in to the scheme at the appropriate level. Most Mathematics schemes take account of a concentric approach where the same topics, developing in sophistication reappear in all four years of the Junior school.

The work outlined above was not designed to cover all aspects implied in the 'Time' theme. It merely shows how children can be involved in discovery, activity and recording. It can serve, too, as a pattern of procedure for further projects on this theme and others.

Sources of information

Books

ADLER, I. and ADLER, R., *Directions and Angles*, Dobson (J).

ASIMOV, *The Clock We Live On*, Abelard-Schumann (J/T).

HOOD, P., *How Time is Measured*, Oxford University Press (J/T).

INGLEBY, T. and TAYLOR, J., *Measuring and Recording*, Longman (I/J).

IRWIN, K. G., *Man Learns to Measure*, Dobson (J).

MARSH, L. G., *Let's Explore Mathematics* (four books), A. and C. Black (I/J).

NAYLOR, A. H., *Time and Clocks* (Study Books), Bodley Head (J).

SMITH, T., *Story of Measurement* (Second Series), Blackwell (J).

Poems

DYMENT, CLIFFORD, 'The Return', *as large as alone*, Macmillan.

CHESTERMAN, HUGH, 'The Grandfather Clock', *Poetry Quest* (It Could Happen To You), Blackie.

FARJEON, ELEANOR, 'J is for Jazz Man', *Junior Voices I*, Penguin and 'School Bell', *Poetry Quest* (All Around You), Blackie.

HUBBELL, PATRICIA, 'Shadows', *Junior Voices I*, Penguin.

MORGENSEN, CHRISTIAN, 'Names of the Months', *Junior Voices IV*, Penguin.

NICHOLSON, NORMAN, 'Pendulum Poets', *as large as alone*, Macmillan.

SUMMERS, HAL, 'Out of School', *Poetry Quest* (All Around You), Blackie.

SWENSON, MAY, 'The Watch', *Junior Voices IV*, Penguin.

10

Red Indians

The aim of this project around the theme 'Red Indians' was to give reading practice and opportunities for recording in art, craft, needlework, music and writing, to give practice in research with books and to extend children's investigations to include another culture and another historical period from their own.

The children were between the ages of eight and nine years. The class was unstreamed. The teacher wanted the children to work in fixed groups. Work cards were not used. The teacher wanted the children to plan their own contributions to the theme within each group.

A wall display put up by the teacher provided the initial stimulus. This consisted of illustrations and reference material taken from old magazines. Other information not readily available to the children because of the difficulty of the text, for example the information contained in Lefarge's' *The North American Indian* was summarized by the teacher in note form and written out on large sheets of cartridge paper. These were mounted with the wall pictures. Reference books relevant to the theme were placed in the book corner (see list, p. 65).

The teacher decided to serialize *Sajo and her Beaver Folk* by Grey Owl. She had picked out five tribes from among the many recorded in eighteenth-century America. She chose these because they showed marked differences in life-style, because they were based in different localities in North America, and because information about them was available in books the children could use. The five tribes chosen were:

The Chilkat, living in north-west USA, made totem poles and built large seagoing canoes to hunt whales. They lived mainly on fish, which they caught by constructing traps near the salmon-spawning grounds of the straits around Vancouver Island. Their love of colour and stylized animal designs on pottery and textiles inspired the children to devise designs of their own.

The Dakota were the nomadic buffalo hunters living on the central plains of North America. They lived in tepees and made articles of buffalo hide. They used sledges called 'travois' and after the Spanish settlement, took to riding horses for which they made elaborate saddles.

The Pueblo Indians (the Hopi tribe) were the most settled of North American Indians. They lived in adobe houses, built in the near-desert regions inland from the Californian coast. They made gardens in the desert and grew maize, which they ground into flour. Bread was baked in outside ovens. Their rituals were concerned with fertility and rain-making. They used dolls for ceremonial purposes. Their weaving and pottery were of fine quality. The Navaho have inherited many of their techniques.

The Seneca lived where New York now stands. They were woodsmen and hunters but also cleared trees to plant crops. These were the Indians familiar to readers of Longfellow's *Hiawatha*. They lived in long houses made of meshed twigs covered with bark. Many of their artefacts were made of birch bark or deerskin like those of the Red Indians in *Sajo and her Beaver Folk*. They wore carved wooden masks on ceremonial occasions and used 'wampum' for transactions and treaties.

The Seminole were the Indians written of by Frank Slaughter. They were swamp dwellers, inhabiting the Everglades of Florida. They prized the feathers of exotic birds which they killed with poisoned darts blown through pipes. They lived in thatched chickees raised above the swamps and kept alligators as pets.

The children elected five tribal chiefs. Each chief selected a tribe to include boys and girls. Thereafter the teacher had regular 'pow-wows' with the chiefs to discuss how work was proceeding. Each group with its chief chose an Indian tribe to study. The assignment for each group was to set up a display of models, paintings and writing to show how the tribe they had chosen lived. The children were encouraged to search for and use, wherever possible, materials actually used by the Indians: feathers, hide, bark and wood. Red Indian motifs were used throughout. Most of the information about the tribes was found in *The World Book Encyclopaedia*, volume 10, and in simpler form in *My First Book of Indians*. Ben Hunt's *Indian Craft and Lore* was a useful source of information about clothing and artefacts.

The project lasted about six weeks. Afternoon sessions were devoted to group work in modelling, painting, needlework and writing explanatory labels. The children programmed their own work here, and the chief supervised it, as well as contributing himself. Each tribe was given wall space and table space on which to display finished work.

As there was little mathematics in the theme, except in making models and in symmetry relating to wigwams, the teacher devoted some of the morning to following the school mathematics scheme and some to reading activities unconnected with the theme. The project provided incidental reading activities and required children to use books. Some of the morning was also given to reading the serial story.

The teacher arranged 'booster' lessons to inject interest into the theme. These lessons sometimes took the form of discussions around ideas and problems thrown up by group work, for example: the nomadic way of life, the place of animals in the lives of Red Indians, the impact of European colonization, lack of written communication but other ways of transmitting messages. One or two sessions were given to making masks in various ways: paper sculpture, papier maché, cloth masks, masks carved from wood. Another session was given to a talk about maize and its importance to Red Indians.

As the project progressed the teacher set up times for free writing. These sessions were handled as class activities to enable the children to share ideas and stimuli and to have a quiet atmosphere in which to 'listen to their thoughts'. Before each free writing session the teacher offered a stimulus: a poem, a piece of music, a picture or a discussion about words. On one occasion the teacher and the children talked about and collected 'dry' words, for example, drought, biscuit, crisp, hard, shattered, fracture, crumbling, flake, sear, whisper, scrape and so on. These provided verbal ammunition when the children wrote about 'Waiting for rain'. On another occasion the teacher read an extract from *The Ghosts of the Buffaloes* by Vachell Lindsay. Ideas and stimuli for free writing came from *Sajo*, for instance 'The forest fire', 'Shooting the rapids'. These stimuli were not intended as models for imitation. Their purpose was twofold: to remind the children of some of the ideas and experiences that had been shared in group work and to offer examples of reflective writing.

Drama was incorporated into this project. The children composed music for ceremonials, hunting, war songs and travelling songs. Dances were performed to this music. Discussions leading to drama centred on such issues as: 'Is it time to move on?' (Dakota), 'White men in the swamps' (Seminole), 'Waiting for rain' (Hopi), 'The Ocean-going canoe has not yet returned' (Chilkat), 'Winter is coming' (Seneca). The children in their 'tribal' groups were given time to discuss these issues from the point of view of the Red Indians. Scraps of dialogue and action emerged from these discussions. The teacher then suggested that the groups prepare acted episodes to present the problem to an audience (consisting of the rest of the class). At some point children had to consider not only the matter of their presentations but the way in which they could be best dramatized, so that these drama discussions had a dual purpose of making children think generally about the nature of dramatic presentation and also further involving them directly in the theme of the project. Where projects are wholly book-based it is necessary to involve the children more directly by activities like drama and free writing. Some of the issues discussed in the drama sessions were also explored in free writing. One informed the other.

The project lasted from the beginning of term to half-term. In the days before half-term, the children tidied their displays and invited children from other classes to come and see what they had done and hear how it had been achieved.

Sources of information

Books

BLACKWOOD, P. E., ed. *North American Indians* and *Winning the West*, Transworld (T/J).

BLEEKER, S., *Indians*, Dent (J) and *The Apache: Raiders of the South West, Horsemen of the Western Plateaux, Navajo* and *The Sioux: The Hunters and Warriors of the Plains*, Dobson (J).

CHILTON, C., *The Book of the West*, Odhams (J).

GORHAM, M., *Red Indians*, Dobson (J).

HOARE, R. J., *The Old West*, Muller (J).

HUNT, B., *Indian Craft and Lore*, Hamlyn (J).

KNIGHT, D., *American Indians*, Patterson Blick (J).

SLADE, R., *Masks and How To Make Them*, Faber (J).

North American Indians in Enc. Britt. The World Book Encyclopaedia, Field Enterprises, vol. 10.

Stories

GREY OWL, *Sajo and her Beaver Folk*.

LONDON, JACK, *White Fang*, New Windmill Series (J).

PERKINS, R., *The Indian Twins*, Cape (I).

RUTGERS VAN DER LOEFF, A., *Children on the Oregon Trail*, Penguin (J).

Songs

MACMAHON, D., *More Songs of the New World* and *Songs of the New World*, McDougall.

SEEGER, R. C., *American Folk Songs for Children*, Doubleday (N.Y.).

Miscellaneous Sources

Pictures from *National Geographic* and *Life* magazines and *Look and Learn*.

The American Museum in Britain, Claverton Manor, Bath, Somerset (Bath 60503) is worth a visit if the school is near enough. The museum may also be able to supply loans of exhibits and reference material.

The John Judkyn Memorial, Freshford Manor, Bath will also lend show-cases of exhibits on American History to schools provided the school will fetch the exhibits from the Museum.

The American Embassy will sometimes send speakers to talk to classes of schoolchildren and will send publicity material in the form of maps and pictures (details of these and other publicity services to schools from 'The Treasure Chest for Teachers).

'Discurio', 9 Shepherd Street, London W1 will loan gramophone records of folk music telling the story of North America.

'The Folk Box' by Electra Records is also a recommended buy for folk songs of the history of North America. Both the 'Discurio' material and 'The Folk Box' material have a range beyond Red Indian history.

I I

Climatic regions

The aim of this project was to give a general view of some aspects of the world's main climatic regions through a study of their geographical location and the plants, animals and primitive societies living in them. It was hoped in this way to lay the foundations of study in more specific topics: 'Cocoa', 'Zoo animals', 'Homes' or 'Cats'. This was a vicarious experience project; through books the children would have experiences of physical environment other than their own. It came at a time when the children's own choice of reading matter showed that they were becoming interested in the world beyond that they could see and explore at first hand.

The study of primitive societies offers children a view of life where problems very like the ones faced in their own society are solved in organized groups which are self-contained and less complex. But no study of primitive peoples should be undertaken for the purely exotic factors in their ways of life. At all times the emphasis should be on the similarities in the needs and problems of people, wherever they live and however sophisticated their cultures.

This was a class of third-year Junior children who had not worked through themes before. The class was unstreamed with some poor readers. The teacher decided to direct the children through a control project on their own region to give them some idea of what was required.

In a series of sessions where they worked mainly, not in small groups, but as a class, the children investigated the following aspects of 'Temperate Regions'.

Temperature and rainfall. The children, using statistics from daily newspapers made graphs to show the temperature and rainfall of various towns in Great Britain, Europe and North America. Statistics were not available for towns in Asia.

Plants. The children made collections of plants which grew in abundance around the school—weeds and garden plants. They visited a market garden and noted what plants were grown without glass. This was the Autumn term and the children were not able to make gardens of their own out of doors, but they made miniature gardens on dinner plates using tiny weeds.

Animals. The children visited the local Natural History Museum to look at the animals which are indigenous to temperate zones. In the classroom they worked in pairs to make a detailed study of the habits and habitats of some of these animals.

The seasons. The teacher gave several class lessons about the sun's relationship to the earth and the affect of that relationship on the seasons, temperature and lengths of day and night. The children collected pictures to typify the appearance of the countryside at different seasons. They visited the local park and made a more detailed study of changes in plant growth specific to Autumn.

Farming. In groups the children studied the types of farming in Great Britain and compared these with farms in New Zealand. Each group took a type of farming and made a model to show a typical farm and field system. This study was superficial and the children looked at only two aspects: space available and used and the soil in relation to crops and livestock. They were able to visit a dairy farm and had visited a sheep farm in the Cotswolds earlier in the year.

Incidental reading

Not all the research was possible at first hand. The teacher introduced the children to the use of reference books. She showed them how to make use of a table of contents and an index, and how to make notes from their reading. She encouraged them to read what several books had to say on the same subject and to record the substances of their researches in their own words. The important point about using books of reference, and one that the teacher was anxious for her pupils to learn, was that these are rarely read from cover to cover like story books.

Writing. The children wrote labels to go with models. They described their visits. On the day of the first hard frost the teacher took the children to the park again. Here they found spiders' webs white with frost, they examined leaves edged with hoar and felt the iron hardness of the ground. They looked for patterns and pictures in the frozen puddles. Back in the classroom the teacher read 'Hard Frost' by Andrew Young, from *Voices I* published by Penguin. The children wrote their own descriptions of a frosty morning.

Story. During this time the teacher read in serial form: *Worzel Gummidge* by Barbara Euphan Todd. In craft sessions the children made models of the scarecrows in the story and painted pictures to illustrate episodes of the tale, but the story also served to reinforce the factual information they had been gathering about farms and the countryside.

Music

After one visit the teacher played a selection of orchestral pieces to the children and asked them to choose the one most evocative of their visit. Most of the children agreed that of the pieces ('Fingal's Cave' by Felix Mendelssohn, part of the suite: 'Scheherazade' by Rimsky-Korsakov, 'Mars' from *The Planets Suite* by Holst and 'The Wasps' by Vaughan-Williams) the last seemed most appropriate.

The class learned the song 'Country Gardens' and composed percussion accompaniments to the Japanese poem: 'The falling leaves fall and pile up: the rain beats on the rain' and 'Whisky Frisky' (about a squirrel) from *Junior Voices I.*

Drama

The teacher set up a discussion topic: Planning a new farm. She gave each group a large outline map of an imaginary area. Features like relief and natural drainage and some roads had been marked in. The basic soil types were indicated simply (clay,

69

clay and gravel, clay with flints, fen, sandy soil, loam, etc.). The children had to decide what kind of crops and livestock they would raise, where fields and farm buildings would be sited, what produce they would market and how they would get it to marketing centres. After several sessions of discussions, during which time the children referred to books for additional information, the groups, one by one, submitted their plans to the rest of the class for their comments.

Drama may seem a misnomer here, but during the discussions children moved easily from talking of 'they' to talking of 'we' or 'I'. The discussions became enactments of possible like discussions of real situations. When the group presented their plans to the rest of the class they talked as though they were the farmers concerned.

This initial project lasted three weeks. The children had begun to show initiative in finding and offering information, in selecting appropriate ways of recording it. They had begun to approach information books critically. They had learned how to set about making and using graphs and they had learned something about their own climatic region as a basis for comparison with others.

The teacher then divided the class into five groups. Each group was given another zone to study: 'Arctic Tundra', 'The Mediterranean Regions', 'The Grasslands', 'The Hot Deserts' and 'Tropical Rain-forests'. Each group was given display space in the classroom or corridors and they were allotted time in the school central library to select books they thought would be of help. The assignments for all groups were the same:

Paint pictures, or make collages to show some of the wild animals of your zone in their natural settings.

Collect plants which are grown indoors or under glass in this country but grow out of doors and wild in the region you are studying. (The Arctic Tundra group could not do this. They collected lichens and mosses.)

Make models to show the homes of people in your region. Choose people who use most closely their natural environments.

Mark your region on a map of the world and show which countries and continents occur in it or partly in it.

Choose gramophone recordings of music which you think describe the atmosphere of the regions you are studying. Compose some music which does this too.

Make an anthology of poems which describe aspects (climate, animals, problems of living) in your region. Write descriptions of your own.

The children in each group shared these assignments. Every child made a painting or collage picture. The children in the group co-operated on models and the plant collection. In spare minutes and during reading time the children sought for poems and copied them out for the anthology. Each child in the group found out about a village in his region and described life there. The teacher encouraged recording in writing, labels for models, descriptions and lists of countries occurring in the zone.

The teacher's contribution at first was organizational. She allotted times when various groups could listen to or make music, she provided a choice of poetry anthologies and gramophone records. She gave advice about materials and demonstrated one or two techniques: how to make wire figures for dressing, wet and dry brush painting, how to mount plant collections. Later she offered poems of her choice for the class's consideration. During this project she read, in serial form *Sammy Going South* by W. H. Canaway (Nelson). This is a story of a small boy who undertakes the journey from Port Said to Johannesburg after his parents have been killed. He crosses Africa from North to South and has many strange encounters.

Some activities were shared by all groups in common. They all listened to the serialized story. When one group wanted to visit the subtropical greenhouses at the Botanic Gardens everybody went along. Times for free writing were structured as follows: one group would talk about its zone and what had been discovered so far. To this the teacher would add a 'booster' (see p. 64) in the form of a poem, passage of descriptive prose or piece of music (see p. 74 lists). Then the whole class would write about some aspect suggested by the stimulus. These free writing efforts were written out 'in rough'. The teacher arranged tutorials with each child during the week, tutorials in which she discussed with children individually problems of effectiveness, punctuation, spelling and grammar. The children copied out their work for display on the wall.

The teacher found it more meaningful to teach punctuation, spelling and grammar in this way. Punctuation and grammar which are often appreciated more by ear than eye were usually corrected by the child himself when he read his written passage to the teacher. The teacher offered general spelling rules and at all times encouraged the use of word lists and dictionaries. This teacher used a wall dictionary. (See description on page 74.) Effectiveness was a point of discussion between teacher and child: what did he want to say? how could he make a reader want to keep on reading? were the words really working hard for him? Sometimes the teacher suggested the use of a more vigorous verb to replace a string of adjectives, for example: instead of 'the huge, tall tree stood in the wood' one might write 'the tree towered over the other trees in the wood'. Tutorials lasted about five minutes each. During tutorial time other children were copying out their writing or choosing poems, reading, working at collage or needle-work pictures or making notes from reference books. The teacher justified the time spent on tutorials in this way. They offered opportunities for one to one conversations with children, English language teaching had purpose in this context, 'a child writing is a child reading' and, as writing is an individual activity, each child's writing should be treated individually.

The teacher also suggested topics for discussion drama. This was usually done during times when the class were timetabled for the use of the school hall, so that the children could disperse into small contained groups for the discussion and could act out some of the results of discussion. Topics suggested for discussion are listed at the end of this chapter.

Lastly the teacher suggested that each group tell the 'story' of its researches in music, poems by other people, in free writing from members of the group and in reference to the wall displays. Each group put together a programme to do this, and pro-grammes were performed to the rest of the class. Time was allowed for questions at the end of each programme. The teacher made private notes of the questions asked. She found that they gave indications of the children's specific interests and suggested the lines future projects might take.

Wall dictionary

A wall dictionary encourages the children to be independent of the teacher in 'word-getting'. When it has been in use for a day or two it releases the teacher from the seemingly endless chore of giving 'spellings'. It prepares children for the techniques of using a printed dictionary. It demonstrates that words are shared and that they embody shared ideas.

A wall dictionary is a series of booklets, one for each letter of the alphabet, or for each symbol used initially if the Initial Teaching Alphabet is used. The booklets should be designed to hang on a row of hooks or to fit into a series of pockets so that they can be removed individually and taken to a desk. The booklets need contain only two or three pages of size about 15 by 10 cm and a cover bearing the initial letter in both upper and lower case. I used coloured card for the cover and two cards below joined by string threaded through holes punched at the top of all three cards. The writing inside the booklets need be only as large as the children's own writing. The pages are blank to begin with.

Words are put into the dictionary:

(*a*) whenever there is an accumulation of words on the blackboard after a lesson or discussion. These are transferred to the appropriate booklets of the dictionary as part of the lesson or discussion so that the children can see them being written in.

(*b*) when children are writing and want word spellings. The child brings the appropriate booklet to the teacher who writes in the word. The child carries the booklet to his desk and copies the word on to his paper (or into his own word book if he has one). The next child who wants this word is referred to the wall dictionary. Very soon most of the common words required by children are in the dictionary, words like 'because', 'while', 'were', 'their', etc.

(*c*) when the teacher notices a child has misspelled a word, he asks the child to fetch the appropriate booklet and he writes down the correct spelling there for the child to copy. Not all children know they are misspelling words and therefore will not ask for spellings. The teacher encourages children to be observant about standard spelling and to check their own attempts, but bears in mind that a child who tries first for himself is worthy of praise.

The wall dictionary is not a magic gateway to correct spelling. Children need to be encouraged to use it and to be taught how to use it. For instance, silent initial letters, e.g. the 'w' in 'write' can be pitfalls. Where children are taught phonics, it is useful to include booklets for words beginning with double consonants like 'ch' and 'th'.

In schools where *Breakthrough to Literacy* is used as a reading system, 'Breakthrough' type folders can be used instead of booklets, but these may take up a great deal of space.

Sources of information

General Books

BETHERS, R., *This Is Our World*, Macmillan (J).

CROMBIE, I., *My Home Series*, Longman (I/J).

DEBENHAM, F., *The World Is Round*, Macdonald (J/T).

DISNEY, WALT, *People and Places*, Purnell (J).

FISHER, M., *A World of Animals*, Brockhampton (J).

HILL, R., *Bushland and Seashore* (for extracts for reading), Lansdowne (T).

HUXLEY, FRANCIS, *People of the World in Colour*, Blandford (J).

RONAN, C. A., *Earth from Pole to Pole*, Harrap (J/T).

SUTHERLAND, E., and SUTHERLAND, K., *Our World in Colour*, Ward Lock (J).

Books about Temperate Zones

ARCHER, A. B., and THOMAS, H. G., *First Geography, Book III*, Ginn (J).

BADMIN, S. R., *Village and Town*, Puffin (J).

CLARK, R. W., *We Go to Scotland* and *We Go to Southern England* and *We Go to the West Country*, Harrap (J).

GAGG, J. C., *Rivers in Britain*, Blackwell (J).

HUNTER, A., *Britain is my Home*, Johnson (J).

HUTCHINGS, M., *What shall I do?* Mills & Boon (J).

KOENIG, M., *Animals At Home*, Chambers (I/J).

LOMAN, A., *Looking at Holland*, Black (J).

MCDONALD, J., *Wales in Pictures*, Oak Tree Press (J).

NACH, J., *England in Pictures* and *Scotland in Pictures*, Oak Tree Press (J).

NADEN, C. J., *Grasslands Around the World*, F. Watts (I/J).

SAUVAIN, M. A., *Exploring at Home*, Hulton (J).

VERITE, MARCELLE, *Gardens Through the Ages*, Odhams (J).

Stories

COCKETT, M., 'The Giant Sunflower', Hamish Hamilton (I/J).

MAYNE, W., 'The Rolling Season,' Hamish Hamilton (J).

TODD, B. E., 'Worzel Gummidge', Penguin (I/J).

Poems

BROWNING, ROBERT, 'Home Thoughts from Abroad', Book of English Verse, Penguin.

ELIOT, T. S., 'New Hampshire', *Words Take Wing Book II*, E. J. Arnold.

FROST, ROBERT, 'After Apple-picking', *Penguin Poets: Robert Frost*, Penguin and 'Gathering Leaves', *Words Take Wing Book II*, E. J. Arnold.

TESSIMOND, A. S. J., 'A Hot Day', ibid.

TODD, B. E., 'The Calendar', ibid.

Filmstrips

'Life in the Autumn' (CGB 416), 'Life in the Spring' (CGB 413), 'Life in the Summer' (CGB 415), 'Life in the Winter' (CGB 417) from Common Ground Filmstrips.

'The Alpine Family' from Hulton Educational Publications Ltd., 55/59 Saffron Hill, London EC1.

Books about Polar Regions and Tundra

BAUM, A. Z., *Antarctica: The Worst Place in the World*, Collier-Macmillan (T).

BLACKWOOD, P., ed. *Polar Regions*, Transworld (T).

BRANLEY, F., *Icebergs* (Let's Read and Find Out), A. and C. Black (I/J).

CROMBIE, I., *My Home in the Frozen North*, Longman (I).
DARBOIS, D., *Achouna, his life in the Arctic*, Chatto & Windus (I/J).
RADCLIFFE, J. T., *Polar Regions*, Muller (J).
SMITH, F. C., *World of the Arctic*, Lutterworth Press (J).
VEVERS, G., *Animals of the Arctic*, Bodley Head (I/J).

Stories
CARSON, R., *Under the Sea Wind*, Panther.
MOWAT, F., *People of the Deer*, Michael Joseph.

Poems
FIELD, RACHEL, 'Something Told by the Wild Geese', *Words Take Wing Book II*, E. J. Arnold.
TRADITIONAL, 'Eskimo Hunting Song', *Junior Voices II*, Penguin.
TRADITIONAL, 'Kayak Paddler's Joy at the Weather', ibid.

Music
WALTON, W., 'Symphony No. I in B flat minor' (first movement).

Filmstrips
'Lapps and Reindeer' from Picture Post, Hulton Press, 43 Shoe Lane, London EC4.
'Penguins' from Daily Mail, School Aid Dept., New Carmelite House, London EC4.

Books about Deserts
BRICK, A. R., *Eli Lives in Israel*, Methuen (J).
DARBOIS, D., *Hassan, his Life in the Desert*, Chatto & Windus (I/J).
EDWARDSON, C., *Miriam Lives in a Kibbutz*, Pergamon (J).
GOETZ, D., *Deserts* (The Background Geographies), Wheaton (J).
HERDMAN, T., *Lands in the Desert* (Colour Geographies), Longman (J).
KAY, S., *The Arab World*, Oxford University Press (T/J).
KNIGHT, C. D., *Deserts*, Kaye & Ward (J).
O'CLEARY, H., *The Nile*, Dobson (J).
POSELL, E., *Deserts*, Muller (J).
SHEARMAN, J., *Iran*, A. and C. Black (J).
STEVENSON, W., *Bushbabies* (Peacock), Penguin (I/J).

THOMPSON, J. L. C., *Animals of the Desert*, Bodley Head (I/J).

WHITE, T., *South of Suez and Panama*, Johnston (J/T).

Stories

BECKLEY, R., *Folk Tales of the World—Australia*, E. J. Arnold.

CALDER, R., *Men Against the Desert*, Allen & Unwin.

CANAWAY, W. H., *Sammy going South*, Nelson. (Fictional journey of a little boy across Africa.)

KINGLAKE, A. W., *Eothen* (extracts), Nelson and *With Kinglake in the Holy Land*, Muller.

SALKEY, A., *Drought*, Oxford University Press

WESTWOOD, G., *Narni of the Desert*, Hamish Hamilton.

Poems

FRY, CHRISTOPHER, 'Rain on a dry ground', *as large as alone*, Macmillan.

STEVENSON, R. L., 'Travel', *Words Take Wing Book II*, E. J. Arnold.

Filmstrips

CALDER, R., 'Water in the Desert' from National Committee for Visual Aids in Education and 'Water for a Thirsty Land' from British Institute Films, Hill Green Road, Mitcham, Surrey.

Books about Tropical Rainforests

CALDWELL, J., *Let's Visit Brazil*, Burke (J).

CAVANNA, B., *Paulo of Brazil*, Chatto & Windus (J).

CROMBIE, I., *The Amazon* (My Home Series), Longman (I).

EGAN, E. W., *Brazil in Pictures*, Oak Tree Press (J).

GOETZ, D., *Tropical Rain Forests*, Wheaton (I/J).

HERRMANS, R., *River Boy: adventure on the Amazon*, Collins (J).

HOKE, H., *Tropical Animals*, Watts (J).

LAND, M. and LAND, B., *Jungle Oil*, Chatto & Windus (J/T).

MATSCHAT, C. H., *Animals of the Valley of the Amazon*, Abelard-Schumann (J).

VERITE, M., *Animals of the Forest*, Chatto & Windus (J).

Stories

ATTENBOROUGH, D., *Zoo Quest to Guiana*, Lutterworth Press.

DURRELL, G., *The Bafut Beagles* and *The Overloaded Ark*, Faber.

FORESTER, C. S., *The African Queen*, Penguin.

GUILLOT, R., *Tom-toms in Oworo*, Collins.

KIPLING, RUDYARD, *Just So Stories*.

Poems

DAVIES, W. H., 'The Rain', *Poetry Quest* (It could happen to you),
 Blackie.

TURNER, W. J., 'India', *Poetry Quest* (Through the Five Senses),
 Blackie.

WEVILL, D., 'Monsoon', *as large as alone*, Macmillan.

Filmstrips
'Rain' (No. G33) from Visual Productions Ltd.

Books about Mediterranean Regions
BAKER, F. N., *Greece*, A. and C. Black (J).

BUCKLEY, P., *Cesare of Italy* and *Luis of Spain*, Chatto & Windus (J).

MARTIN, R., *Looking at Italy*, A. and C. Black (J).

ROWLEY, H., *Student's Bible Atlas*, Lutterworth Press (J/T).

Stories

GALLICO, P., *A Small Miracle*, Michael Joseph.

Music
BIZET, Overture to Carmen.

MOZART, Italian Caprice Opus 45, Decca-Ace of Clubs
Spanish Guitar Music.

I 2

1066 and All That

This project was planned in advance, as shown in the diagram on p. 89, and modified as it developed in practice. Members of the class were divided into groups as follows: the teacher selected three leaders who were then called Harold Godwinsson, Harold Hardrada and William of Normandy. As these were boys, the teacher evened the score by choosing three girls to be their counsellors. Counsellors and 'kings' then chose the rest of the group.

Illustrative material, some maps and panels bearing brief historical details had already been mounted on one wall. The wall space was divided into three areas and each group was assigned an area where they could mount their own displays as the project proceeded. Work cards were also in three groups. A colour coding was used; backing paper for wall displays, and the card on which assignments were written were of three colours, a colour per group.

On one afternoon work cards were given out and the children allowed time to discuss these with one another. Work cards were:

Saxons

A. Draw a map to show the extent of the Saxon kingdom in England. Include the English Channel and the coast of Normandy.
B. Dress a doll as a Saxon lord.
C. Dress a doll as a Saxon lady.

D. Dress a doll as a Saxon peasant (male).
E. Dress a doll as a Saxon peasant woman.
F. Make a model of a typical Saxon village. Include fields.
G. Make a model of a Saxon shield. Try to use materials (and techniques) actually used.
H. Make a banner for Harold Godwinsson.
I. Copy some Saxon designs and use them in embroidery or tapestry.
J. Find out distances in English miles, and also kilometres, from London to Stamford Bridge and from London to Senlac.

Normans

A. Dress a doll as a Norman soldier.
B. Dress a doll as a Norman lord.
C. Dress a doll as a Norman lady.
D. Make a model of a Norman shield. Try to use materials (and techniques) actually used.
E. Find out how chain mail was made. Try to make some.
F. Make a model of a Norman ship.
G. Design and make a banner for William of Normandy.
H. Draw a map of the Senlac area and make a plan of battle order. Show by means of arrows what happened during the battle.
I. Compose some music for a battle.

Vikings

A. Dress a doll as a Viking warrior.
B. Make a model of a Viking village.
C. Dress a doll as a Viking peasant woman.
D. Make a model of a Viking longship.
E. Draw a map to show the Viking lands and the coast of Britain nearest to them.
F. Make a map to show the route of the Vikings to York and Stamford Bridge.
G. Design a sail motif for Harold Hardrada's ship.

H. What means of navigation did the Vikings use? Prepare a talk about these for the class (with illustrations).
I. Make a Viking shield.

Some work cards were given to children individually, some to pairs, but children soon formed other groups round activities and books.

When the children had discussed the work cards, the class went to the school library to choose books needed for the topic. The books were brought down to the classroom and the children spent the rest of the afternoon looking at and making notes from them, and discussing with the teacher the materials they would need. During this session the teacher showed the children what was available in the way of material and equipment, encouraged them to make notes and diagrams before they started models, established liaison between children whose assignments overlapped and made notes about any reference material not immediately available. After school she took a group of children down to the local public library to look for more reference books. These she was able to borrow on a termly loan. The children who had gone with her to the library made themselves responsible for listing these books and looking after them for the period of the project. Children also brought from home, books and illustrative material from comics and magazines.

The work on this project occupied most afternoons. The mornings were spent in following the school mathematics scheme and in activities like PE, games and swimming. The afternoon following the giving out of work cards, was spent in making a start on models and other responses to work cards. Some children had spent the previous book session reading the books available without much direction. The teacher did not discourage this practice. These children were often the ones who knew later where specific information could be found. The speed at which the children worked and the speed at which they got down to their activities varied from group to group. While the teacher was concerned for each child to start on something specific as soon as possible, she allowed the children to make their own pace at first, only occasionally offering suggestions on ways to speed up operations. One of her main concerns here was that children should use books of information with efficiency. She showed them how to make efficient notes without too much writing and she also showed that a diagram is often a good way of recording information.

The desks in the classroom were arranged in groups of six or eight to make flat working tops. Each afternoon these were laid out as working areas: two modelling tables, a drawing table, a table for those who were consulting books, and a 'wet' table. Later a clay table was made for children who had decided to make clay figures instead of wire models of dolls, and a painting table for children who had reached a painting stage. An area where needlework could be done was made in the corridor, and the book table became a writing table for the writing of explanatory labels for finished work.

The children making models of ships wanted to make these to scale. Dimensions for a Viking ship were available and the children started to make plans. The teacher offered some lessons about scale during the morning mathematics sessions and these linked with the assignments of the map makers. Eventually almost the whole class was drawn into the activity of those who were making a battle plan, and the teacher suggested that the two leaders concerned should sort this out between themselves and report to the rest of the class. At the end of afternoon sessions there was time to discuss problems and to look at what had been done so far. Time was made for various children to tell the class about their researches. One session was given to the child who had prepared a talk on Viking navigation. During sessions like these the children also mentioned fiction books about the period and the teacher read extracts from these. Rudyard Kipling's *Puck of Pook's Hill*, which had lain neglected in the class fiction library suddenly became popular in this way and the teacher needed to obtain more copies of it.

The teacher herself offered class lessons to fill in the history of the period, and 'booster' material (see p. 65). During this time the headmaster brought in a newspaper which was being issued by Hastings Corporation to commemorate the Battle of Hastings. It was written as though produced at the time. The children wished to produce such a newspaper themselves. Other work was halted while this was organized.

The children first decided what would go into the newspaper. They went further than the Hastings edition and suggested the inclusion of such things as cookery and fashion articles and horoscopes. The next discussion was about the kind of jobs needed to produce a newspaper. The children elected a pair of editors, who chose a staff of reporters, artists, compositors and printers. The work for the newspaper was done mainly in children's spare moments. The newspaper was to be of eight pages. Eight large sheets of drawing paper were pinned to a wall in the corridor (by this time there was no more wall space in the classroom) and the editors decided what should go on each page. They 'commissioned' some articles, others they sifted from children's contributions. They used one or two pieces from the children's free writing sessions, but the editors were not too satisfied with the immediacy of these. At last one of the editors wrote a front page article in 'journalese':

'In one fell blow England lost her freedom. Today a country is conquered. All England mourns the death of our king. It was on a Saturday that he lost his life. An arrow fired by the treacherous Normans hit him in the eye. It was early morning when the horns first rang out. All I could see from my vantage point were hundreds of armoured Normans. Although not so impressive the Saxon lines were just as grim. Then with a roar of battle-cries almost equalling a thunderclap, the Normans charged. But they were repelled again and again. When the day was nearly spent Harold received his fatal wound. With this the English lost heart and after hours of hard fighting the battle was terminated and all that was left of our sovereign was a mass of flesh and bones' (Stephen, aged $9\frac{1}{2}$ years).

Christine suggested a cheap dish in her cookery article. It used ducklings from razed Saxon homesteads with 'looted apples to follow'.

The editors selected an 'artist' from the class to design a cover, and a boy who had talent in lino-cutting produced some designs to fill in odd spaces in the newspaper. As work came in, it was pinned to the appropriate page. The editors and editorial staff spent a day arranging and editing copy. Another group of children then rewrote the pages on to duplicating skins and the 'printers' duplicated these under the watchful eye of the school secretary. Illustrations, on lino blocks, were added, and the pages stapled together. A distribution team sold the newspapers to children around the school and when the paper and other materials had been paid for, enough money was left to buy a book for the school library. All the children in the class were actively involved at some time on the newspaper (the distribution team included non-readers) and the whole operation was undertaken alongside other project work. Making a 'newspaper' became part of the repertoire to be included in other projects.

After a week of group activity sessions, interspersed with discussions and some readings, it became obvious that the children were becoming partisan about their study of Saxons, Normans and Vikings. They used to call out battlecries in the playground and stage mock battles. This gave the teacher the idea of incorporating their enthusiasm into a play. The play would take the form of scenes enacted either by the children directly or through puppets (a group of children were making puppets to represent the major historical figures of this period, under the guidance of an art student who was attached to the class for teaching practice). These scenes were to be linked by music and choral chants.

One afternoon the teacher set up conditions for composing music. The school had a selection of rhythm and pitched instruments, some bought, some 'home-made'. The class had been following the BBC Schools Radio programme, 'Music Workshop', and were familiar with devising rhythms and simple melodies in the pentatonic scale. One difficulty was that when we used the instruments we disturbed other classes. The teacher found four places round the school where four groups of 'musicians' could work disturbing no one. These were the class stockroom, the medical room, the school greenhouse and a landing on a little-used staircase. Times were chosen for music sessions when other classes were at the playing fields or swimming baths. On these days, the class in groups discussed and devised compositions on various themes. Compositions consisted of a melody on a pitched instrument (xylophone, glockenspiel, recorder or chime-bars) and a rhythmic accompaniment. Groups polished their compositions at play-times and dinner-times. They were encouraged to record their compositions in notation.

There were three groups in connection with the '1066' project. Their briefs were to compose some music for a battle, a funeral procession, a coronation procession, rowing music and music for the dawn of a day of battle.

When the play was put together, it was found to be more effective as a 'heard' play rather than a 'seen' one. This was because the music and the children's own descriptive writing seemed more evocative of events than visual representation, perhaps because more was required of the audience's imaginations. Passages from children's own descriptive writing were substituted for the action. The whole was then tape-recorded and played through the school's recording system to other classes. The puppeteers performed their play to the class on another occasion.

The play and the newspaper successfully collated the work around the theme, with the wall display. The project lasted six weeks and came to an end with the end of term.

Assessment

Most of the work planned for the project was covered in the six weeks (see planning diagram, p. 89). The teacher was able to incorporate the play, which had arisen as an opportunity during the work. As the mathematics in this project was sketchy, the class had a daily mathematics lesson of three-quarters of an hour. This was devoted to a subsidiary theme of 'Linear measurement and scale'. The class measured widths of bays, doorways and windows in the school and tried to determine whether there were standard measurements for these. Using information from Thyra Smith's *The Story of Measurement*, the children discovered standard measurements used by the Saxons and Normans and compared these with present ones. Children making models of homesteads made these to scale. They also discovered that the length of a Viking longship was the same as a canal narrow boat. The class visited a nearby canal to look at a narrow-boat. This helped them to form an impression of the cramped conditions in which the crew of a Viking ship laboured.

Pictures from the Bayeux Tapestry helped to fill in details. Assuming that, as the Normans were of Viking stock, their ships were like Viking ships, the children tried to discover from the tapestry pictures, how many men a ship would carry, how many horses. One picture from the tapestry showed a ship carrying eight men and ten horses.

These investigations were incidental to the work done from assignment cards, but no less important. Sometimes the whole class discussed such problems, sometimes a group worked on them. One child found out details of the D-day invasion fleet in the 1939–45 war and gave a talk on this to the rest of the class. The teacher used frames from a filmstrip on the Bayeux Tapestry to reinforce the discussion. (For details of Bayeux Tapestry reproductions and filmstrip see list.)

The children's interests modified the progress of the project. An interest in the domestic life of the period waned in favour of battles so that the class's discoveries were sketchy in the former area.

The purpose of a project is not to amass facts. Some facts are necessary to inform activities and to give the imagination a framework to work on, but the overall aim of any project is to give children continuing practice in reading, writing, learning to find out, solving problems and learning to co-operate with one another as a community.

Sources of information

General Books

ALLEN, A., *Story of the Village*, Faber (T/J).

BOWOOD, R., *Our Land in the Making: Book* 1, Ladybird (I/J).

ELLIS, A. W., *Life in England: Early and Medieval Times*, Blackie (J/T).

GAGG, J. C., *People through the Years*, Chatto & Windus (J).

GILES, C. W. S., *Looking at Heraldry*, Dent (T).

HASSALL, W. O., *They saw it happen: 55 B.C. to* 1485, Blackwell (J/T).

MUNTZ, H., *Battles: 1066*, Dent (J).

PALMER, M., *Warfare*, Batsford (J/T).

QUENNELL, M., *Everyday Life in Roman and Anglo-Saxon Times*, Batsford (T).

UNSTEAD, R. J., *Story of Britain: Before the Norman Conquest*, Transworld (J).

WARREN, W. L., *The Year of Three Kings: 1066*, Lutterworth Press (J/T).

General Craft Books
MALLEY, A. B., *Project Modelling*, Harrap (J/T).
MARGETT AND SEPTIMA, *Child's Play*, Dent (T).
PLUCKROSE, H., *Art and Craft Today*, Evans (T).

Books about the Normans
DEMPSEY, M. and SHEEHAN, A., *Knights and Castles* (First Library), Macdonald (I/J).

DENNY, S., *Bayeué Tapestry: the story of the Norman Conquest*, Collins (J).

GRAY, P., *The Battle of Hastings*, McGraw-Hill (J).

HODGES, C. W., *The Norman Conquest*, Oxford University Press (J).

LUCKOCK, E., *William the Conqueror*, Wheaton (J).

Books about the Vikings
BURLAND, C. A., *The Vikings*, Hulton (J).

DOLAN, E. M., *Einar the Viking*, A. and C. Black (I/J).

ELLIS, J. and NEURATH, M., *The Vikings* (They lived like this), Macdonald (J).

REEVES, M., *The Vikings* (Then and There series), Longman (J).

SELLMAN, R. R., *The Vikings*, Methuen (T).

SOBOL, D. J., *Barbarian Invaders*, F. Watts (J).

UNSTEAD, R. J., *From Cavemen to Vikings*, A. and C. Black (I/J).

Stories
MUNTZ, H., *Battles: 1066* and *Battles for the Crown*, Dent.
HEYER, G., *The Conqueror*, Pan (J).
KIPLING, RUDYARD, *Puck of Pook's Hill*, Macmillan
SUTCLIFFE, R., *The Lantern Bearers* and *Sword at Sunset*, Oxford University Press (J).

Poems

ANON, 'The Battle of Maldon', 'The Fight at Finnsburg' and
'The Seafarer' (extracts) from *Earliest English Poems*, Penguin.

KIPLING, RUDYARD, 'Harp Song of the Danish Women', 'Puck's
Song', 'Sir Richard's Song' from *Puck of Pook's Hill*, Macmillan.

Filmstrips

'The Saxons' (P.D.5) and 'The Vikings' (P.D.6) from Visual
Productions Ltd.

'William the Conqueror' (Series F561 Ladybird) from Wills &
Hepworth Ltd.

Teacher's planning

The class to be divided into three groups — Saxons, Normans and Vikings

Book on the wall
Reference material divided into 'Saxons', 'Normans' and 'Vikings'
Children's work with labels. Maps etc.

Story
Hope Munzt *Battles for the Crown: 1066* Chatto and Windus
Extracts from:
Georgette Heyer *The Conqueror* Heinemann
Rudyard Kipling *Puck of Pook's Hill* Macmillan
Walter Scott *Ivanhoe* Collins
Charles Kingsley *Hereward the Wake* Collins
'Battle of Maldon' from *Earliest English Poems* Penguin

Reading
Reference books (See list)
Fiction (See list)

Writing
Labels for work
Narrative accounts of battles etc.
Narrative/imaginative — newspaper articles

Art and Craft
Paintings depicting events
Models of homesteads, tools, weapons, ships
Dolls dressed to show clothes, armour
Needlework pictures using characteristic motifs & stitches
Tapestry
Clay figures based on Norman carved chessmen
Puppets

History
The events of the years 1065 — 1066 leading to the Battle of Hastings
Visits to local museum, Norman church

'1066 AND ALL THAT'

Geography
Countries involved and their geographical relation to one another
Scale and distance
Agriculture, trade, transport & communication of the time compared with present day
Relief — use of natural features for defence

Drama
Scenes from events of, 1065/6, e.g.:
'Harold's oath before William'
'The coronation of Harold'
'The exchange between Saxons & Vikings at Stamford Bridge'
Running commentaries on battles. William's disembarkation at Pevensey, etc.

Mathematics
Saxon measurements used in building [e.g. 1 bay = 16 feet (4·8 metres)] and comparison with standard measurement used in building today
Distances travelled
Stresses with reference to castle keeps. Practical testing in P.E. lesson

Music
'Atmospheric' music for battles and processionals, (children's own compositions)
Selections (by children) from recorded music to be used in connection with drama (See list)

Teacher's preliminary planning, to be modified in light of progress and opportunities arising during project

13

A Literature Project

Even when children can read quite well, they still enjoy being read to. Some projects can have as their central focus a work of fiction which is read at intervals by the teacher to the class. *The Summer Birds* by Penelope Farmer was used in this way with a class of third-year Juniors of mixed ability. The book was chosen for its interest for children of this age, its literary merit and its possibilities in providing starting points for the children's investigations and creativity. The book was read during the Spring term. Although the teacher did not know it at the time, the interest it aroused and the increased observation it fostered, was to carry over into field studies the following term.

The story is of a visit of a strange boy to a village school. He teaches the children to fly and tells them they will have this power for a whole summer. The children explore their newfound ability and fly further and further afield as the summer progresses. A note of discord is introduced when the children divide into two factions: some stay with the strange boy, others follow a rival leader, one of the boys at the school. A mock battle in the air is arranged to determine supremacy. The boy stays with the children the whole summer, but when it is time for him to go he tries to persuade some of the children to fly away with him. The story ends on a note of sadness as the boy disappears and the children are earthbound once more.

Penelope Farmer handles her material with sensitivity. The language is simple but evocative, the characterization deftly handled to awaken children's sympathy. The moment in the story when the schoolmistress finds out that the children can fly, but realizes she is too old to learn herself, is poignant, and illustrates the gulf between the world of children and the world of adults.

Teacher's planning

The teacher made herself familiar with the book and divided it into passages to give about twenty minutes reading per session. These sessions were in the first part of the afternoon and were usually followed by some active work connected with the theme of flying.

The reading corner contained reference books about flying and other stories about birds, flying and so on (see p. 000). The teacher also found some poems and prose passages which would reinforce the theme:

EDWIN MORGAN, 'The Starlings in George Square' (first verse), *Junior Voices II*, Penguin.

KIRKUP, JAMES, 'In a Sailplane', *Junior Voices IV*, Penguin.

SWENSON, MAY, 'Feel like a Bird', *Junior Voices IV*, Penguin.

SCRIVEN, R. C., 'Cloud Clipper', *Poetry Quest—Magic Question, Magic Answer*, Blackie.

HOROVITZ, FRANCES, 'Bird', *Children of Albion*, Penguin.

HOPKINS, GERARD MANLEY, 'The Windhover', *Faber Book of Modern Verse*, Faber.

MUIR, EDWIN, 'The Bird', *Selected Poems*, Faber.

Group activities connected with the theme

Bird watching (see A Feather, p. 31):
    Watching and recording flight patterns of birds.
    Watching and recording bird visitors to school area.
Making and sorting a collection of feathers.
Finding pictures of birds in flight and finding poems or quotations from poems to go with them.
Making an anthology of 'Bird' poems and descriptions in prose of birds in flight.

Art and craft activities

Collage pictures of birds in flight
Turning flight patterns into designs for needlework
Making paper sculpture or wire and paper models of birds
Clay models
Mobiles
Paintings of birds in flight
Paintings of scenes from the story

Suggested subjects for drama and movement

Flying, swooping, gliding
Hunting for wildfowl
The movement of the sea at high and low tide
Watching a balloon ascent
A parachute jump
Leaves in the wind
Starlings finding a roost at evening
Discussion points leading to drama:
  The children practising flight. Discussion of whether to tell the
  teacher they can fly.
  Planning the strategy of the air battle.
  What happens at the end of the summer? Do we go with the
  boy or not?
  Where can we fly to?

Music as stimulus for dance and writing

'Don Quixote—Wind Variation', Richard Strauss
'Swan Lake—The Lake and Swan Music', Tschaikovsky
'Overture—The Hebrides—Fingal's Cave', Mendelssohn
'Overture to the Flying Dutchman', Wagner
'L'Aprés Midi d'un Faun', Debussy
'The Swan—Carnival of Animals', Saint-Saens
'Chanson de Matin', Elgar
'Suite—The Wasps', Vaughan Williams
'The Planets—Mercury', Holst

Suggested subjects for free writing

I can fly
Seagulls
The world from the air
Clouds
A battle
Geese at dusk
Lessons on a hot summer's day
What I do on Saturdays in Summer
A balloon journey
A parachute jump

Assessment

The group activities and the art and craft activities were started with the story. The dance, drama and free writing was done when points in the story appropriate to the 'subject' had been reached. Music and poetry were used as stimulus for free writing, but, of course the writing was also informed by the other activities and by the vocabulary of the theme which had arisen in discussions and activities.

When the children wrote about 'The world from the air' some of them became interested in birds-eye views. This led to some work on the difference between maps and photographs taken at ground level. The book *Our World from the Air* was used; Aerofilms produce a similar book of aerial photographs. Work on plan and map-making was developed and this formed a second set of activities when the activities around birds were completed.

A project on the history of powered flight followed this theme, comprising the making of models of flying machines and a frieze to show the sequence in history of their appearance, and also making scale models of modern aircraft from plastic kits. This led to work on reading instructions and scale. The children took parts of the plastic models and using the information provided in the kits drew these parts to actual size on the school playground. A typical question which initiated this work was: 'How many children can stand on the tail-plane of a VC10?'

Other books for literature projects

The Odyssey retold by Barbara Leonie Pickard (Oxford University Press; 9 to 11-year-olds).

This is part of Homer's *Odyssey*, namely the stories Odysseus himself tells of his adventures on the way home from Troy. It contains stories like: 'The bag of winds', 'The Cattle of the Sun', 'The Lotus-eaters', 'Polyphemus', 'Scylla and Charybdis', 'Circe's Island'. Not all these stories need be taken. Each forms a complete unit.

Another Odyssey story which repays project work is the story of Odysseus's return to Ithaca and the battle with the suitors.

The Seagull by Penelope Farmer (Hamish Hamilton; 7 to 9-year-olds).

A boy tends a wounded seagull. This is a short book, suitable for extended treatment like that described around 'The Summer Birds', but for a younger age range.

The Borrowers by Mary Norton (Puffin; 7 to 9-year-olds).

In my opinion this is the best of the 'Borrower' books, certainly from the point of view of project treatment. It gives rise to models and free-writing and some maths in making maps and plans and in scale-drawing.

The Wheel on theSchool by Meindert de Jong (Puffin; 9 to 11-year-olds).

This book, serialized, would fit into a project on 'Wheels' or 'Birds'. Children of a Dutch village wish to encourage storks to nest on the roof of the school. The roof is too steep, but a suitably placed wheel would provide a ledge for a nest. The story is the children's search for a suitable wheel. This story is used from time to time in the BBC Schools Radio Programme 'Living Language'.

The Singing Hill by Meindert de Jong (Lutterworth; 9 to 11-year-olds) is a story of a boy living in a maize growing area of USA who adopts a horse. Used in BBC Schools Radio Programme: 'Living Language'.

Sand by William Mayne (Oxford University Press; 9 to 11-year-olds).

Some boys from the local secondary school find enormous bones in the sand-dunes that are encroaching on the outskirts of the town. They reassemble the bones in the playground of the girls' grammar school, using a disused single track railway to transport the bones. This story has many facets and would link with work on erosion and sedimentation, railways, fossils (especially dinosaurs), and anatomy.

The Rolling Season by William Mayne (Oxford University Press; 9 to 11-year-olds).

A Wiltshire village is short of water in the summer. The wells dry up. An old story tells that the place to dig a well is at the end of the run when a wheel is rolled down a hill. But where to start the rolling from, is a problem. This story would link with work on wheels, water-supply, rivers and wells. (I find that children enjoy William Mayne's books when they are read to them, but find them hard going to read for themselves.)

Drought by Andrew Salkey (Batsford; 9 to 11-year-olds).

This and Andrew Salkey's other books, *Hurricane* and *Earthquake* can be linked with projects on the same themes.

Stig of the Dump by Clive King (Longman; 7 to 9-year-olds).

This is a story for all 'cave-man' enthusiasts.

This list is by no means exhaustive but comprises books which have been tried and found successful as a basis for project work.

Sources of information

Books

ARDLEY, N., *How Birds Behave*, Hamlyn (J).

BOWOOD, R., *The Story of Flight*, Ladybird (I/J).

DEMPSEY, M. and WATERS, F., *Birds* (Junior Reference Library), Macdonald (J).

FRIELING, H., *Birds* (Young Specialist), Burke (T).

(See also booklist for 'Feathers and Flight', page 00.)

Stories

CARSON, R., *Under the Sea Wind* (extracts), Staples Press.

FARMER, P., *The Summer Birds*, Chatto & Windus.

GALLICO, P., *The Snow Goose*, Michael Joseph.

WHITE, T. H., *The Goshawk*, Collins and *The Sword in the Stone*, Collins.

Poems

BRYANT, W. C., 'To a Waterfowl', *Penguin Book of English Verse*, Penguin.

ELIOT, T. S., 'Cape Cod', ibid.

FROST, ROBERT, 'Come In', *Robert Frost: Penguin Poets*, Penguin.

HOPKINS, GERARD MANLEY, 'Windhover', *Faber Book of Modern Verse*, Faber.

HUGHES, TED, 'Thrushes', ibid.

WATKINS, V., 'The Feather', *Selected Poems*, Faber.

Music

Delius, *On Hearing the First Cuckoo in Spring*.

MESSIAEN, *The Awakening of the Birds*.

MOZART, extracts from *The Magic Flute*.

SAINT-SAENS, 'Cocks and Hens' from *Carnival of Animals*.

STRAUSS, 'Wind Variation' from *Don Quixote*.

STRAVINSKY, extracts from *The Firebird*.

TSCHAIKOVSKY, extracts from *Swan Lake*.

14

Opportunities

While themes for many topics are decided and the overall spread of the project worked out in advance, where the timetable is flexible and the children accustomed to working informally, it is possible to use opportunities which arise spontaneously, to initiate projects.

The following projects described are projects which arose from opportunities which had not been foreseen. Some of them, like the 'Snow' theme, lasted only a day, and a longer project was set aside temporarily to make room for this. Others represent themes which were explored in one or two aspects only, alongside other projects.

'Metamorphosis' was taken up as a subsidiary theme when children were working on the theme 'The School Environment'. It provided opportunities for art and free-writing not fully covered by the larger project.

'Ben Hur' (p. 101) began as a supplementary project but developed into a full-scale one.

Snow

It had been snowing all night. The children woke to the perennial wonder of a world transformed. They could think and talk of nothing else. As a calming activity the teacher set them to design snowflakes by using geometric forms. Several children tried to isolate snowflakes so that they could study their shapes, but as the flakes melted quickly the teacher found some photographs of

97

snowflakes in a BBC pamphlet for the programme 'Junior Science'.

While the children were designing snowflakes, the teacher cleared a wall panel to take any contributions to the theme 'Snow'.

Meanwhile one child had come up with the idea of basing her snowflake design on a hexagon. She was set to explain this to the rest of the class and everybody drew and cut out 'snowflakes'. These were used to decorate the wall.

After this the class held a discussion about snow. The children felt that snow must be frozen water but were puzzled because it did not look like ice. The teacher reminded them that when they made snowballs the snow sometimes turned into ice. A child was sent out to fill a clean jam-jar with snow. It was left to melt. When it had melted two things were observed: that the level of water was less than the level of snow (the melted snow took up less space) and that there were grains of grit at the bottom of the jam-jar. The level of water from the melted snow was marked with a sliver of adhesive-backed paper on the side of the jam-jar. The teacher then set a group of children to repeat this activity several times. Was there always the same amount of water from a full jam-jar of snow? What caused the difference in volume? The group were asked to record their observations and suggest explanations.

Another group went to the library to research into the nature of snow. A group settled around the clay table to make models of people using snow for games and sports. Another group painted the same subject.

There had been no play because of the snow, so in the afternoon the teacher took the whole class out to make snowmen. The finished snowmen were inspected to decide on the best and then the children pelted their snowmen with snowballs. This is an improvement on children pelting one another, at least on school premises.

The class came into school again and as soon as they had dried out and warmed up, the teacher read an extract from Scott's 'Journal of his expedition to the South Pole' and Thomas Hardy's 'Snow in the Suburbs'. The children had a choice of ideas for writing, the menace of snow or its beauty. After the experience in the playground some of them were more aware of the discomfort of being cold and wet than of any pleasure in playing with the snow, and these children wrote feelingly from this point of view.

Paintings and writing both descriptive and factual were mounted on the wall. Clay models, drying out, were labelled and displayed beneath the wall display. The children who had been finding out about snow gave a 'lesson' to the rest of the class. The books they had found useful were also displayed.

Although the following day, the current project work was resumed, the 'Snow' display stayed up for several days and children added to it with pictures and information found at home.

Spirals

Cynthia brought to school a spray of some species of climbing vetch which had spiral tendrils on it. The class discussed the use of these tendrils and why they were this shape. The teacher asked the class to keep an eye open for other spiral shapes in nature and in man-made objects. A table was cleared to receive the collection.

The teacher showed the class how to cut a spiral from a circle. These were decorated with writing patterns or words about spirals and hung up in the classroom as mobiles. Discussion about these shapes elicited the response that perhaps spirals were circles moving through time and space.

During the next few days, children brought in screws (which provided thought for a lesson on slopes), a fir-cone, a head of sunflower seeds and shells (which provoked discussion on growth). The children looked for growth lines on snail shells. The teacher mentioned the double helix, the shape of DNA, and would willingly have left the subject there, but spirals cropped up in paintings, in dance and in writing for several months after this.

Metamorphosis

Lynne brought a tin full of cabbage-white caterpillars to school. Her father, a keen gardener thought they were better at school than on his cabbages. A piece of turf bearing some long grass stems was placed at the bottom of an empty aquarium (no longer used because it leaked at the seams). The grass was sprinkled with water and the caterpillars tipped into the vivarium (which the aquarium had now become). Cabbage leaves were begged daily from the kitchen and the caterpillars thrived. During the next few days the caterpillars began to pupate. Soon there were caterpillars at all stages of pupation: some half-changed, some fully changed but still twitching, some beginning to turn yellow and dry. Several caterpillars escaped, although the vivarium was covered with a piece of fine meshed fabric (two hairnets, one over the other, were found fairly efficient for this purpose). The escaping caterpillars hung themselves from the loudspeaker in the classroom to pupate. Only one escaped the cleaners' feather dusters.

With all this activity in the classroom, the children found it hard to concentrate on anything else. Some children had not been aware, before this time, of the process whereby caterpillars turn into butterflies. The teacher found some pictures of caterpillars and butterflies and pinned these around the vivarium.

John brought in a 'woolly-bear' caterpillar which obligingly buried itself in the turf of the vivarium to pupate. Here was a difference. Some caterpillars pupated above ground, some under the soil. The children remembered other pupae found in the bark of trees or wrapped in cocoons of fine silk.

The teacher read the extract from *The Water Babies* by Charles Kingsley, where Tom meets the dragon-fly nymph. Some children went fishing, failed to find any dragon-fly nymphs, but they did gather caddis worms which were put into the cold water aquarium.

In drama period the children tried to 'burst out of their skins'. It was in this lesson that the word 'Metamorphosis' was first used. The word captured the children's imagination.

One afternoon, the teacher got out the large bag of 'bits' (fabric, string, decorative papers, threads, fibres, wrappings of all sorts) which was used for collage work. She asked the children what materials they would use if they wanted to make a dragon-fly. It did not matter that the right kind of materials were not always to hand; the discussion about the qualities required in those materials produced words to describe dragonflies in metaphoric terms. Thick woollen cloth was too 'heavy', 'soft', 'deadening', wood was too 'solid' and 'stiff', wings might be made of 'organdie' but something 'metallic' and 'transparent' would be better. Bodies would need to be 'thin', 'twiggy', 'wiry'.

The children settled down to make dragonflies. The teacher bought a large bag of toffees wrapped in cellophane and metallic papers. The children ate the sweets and used the papers. The dragonflies were hung on fine wire across the classroom where they sparkled in the sunlight. Those that had wings made of acetate sheeting made interesting reflected light patterns on the ceiling. All this the class enjoyed and talked about.

Later the vocabulary which had arisen during discussion and model-making was used by the children to write about 'Metamorphosis'. The poem 'Was Worm' by May Svenson, from *Voices I* was read by the teacher as a booster, but some children remembered tadpoles kept in the Spring and wrote about thsee One girl wrote about eggs hatching.

Subjects for craft, drama and free-writing hinged on this theme for one week, but the theme was later used as inspiration for needlework designs.

Caterpillars are going to be brought into the classroom in May and June of every year. It is a good idea to have a vivarium already set up to receive them, and a few pictures and information books ready for the invasion.

Ben Hur

Timothy brought a recording of the incidental music to the film *Ben Hur*. We had been using recorded music as a stimulus for expressive writing, and this composition had a magnificent 'rowing' sequence. As soon as the teacher played this to the children they began to make rowing movements. She told the class briefly about Roman galleys and that the rowers would be slaves, chained to the oars. A hortator would keep time with a drum. Then the class went down to the hall where there was more space.

In the hall, the teacher set up two banks of rowers. One boy took a drum and became hortator. Some of the girls elected to be waves at each side of the ship. The music was played again.

The following day, with books from the school library and some pictures, the class began to research into the background of the 'Ben Hur' story. One group found out about Roman galleys, another about Roman soldiers, another about the Roman Empire at the time of the birth of Christ, another about chariot-racing. The children made their own choices as to the group they wished to join and at this time the teacher left the organization and response very much to them, arbitrating occasionally when a group was too large or arguments about responsibilities arose. She also made suggestions about the way responses should be recorded, but this was a class who had worked in this way several times before and most children knew what was appropriate. The teacher cleared wall space and mounted some of the illustrative material. Books were displayed below. The children brought a great deal of reference material from home on this occasion.

The teacher also got hold of a copy of Lew Wallace's *Ben Hur*, acquainted herself with the story and read or told extracts to the children. The music was listened to again and again, and during movement periods in the hall other sequences—slaves driven through the desert on their way to the galleys, a Roman triumph —were added to the 'rowing' sequence. The boys who had a craft period while girls took needlework with a visiting needlework specialist, made themselves costumes as Roman soldiers. These were made of sugar paper for quickness but much research was done into materials actually used and the ways the clothing and armour were actually made.

Alongside the *Ben Hur* story is the story of Christ. After a class discussion about the three kings who visited Jesus, each child wrote a description of the journey as though he were one of the kings:

I, Balthasar an Egyptian, left my land and towering buildings for something I am not quite sure of. The ships bounded up and down like hapless logs, waves crushed the deck as I made the journey across the Red Sea. My gift was gold but it did not seem enough for a king. Now I have a journey across a hot desert. Wind rushes through me and blinds my tired eyes but still I go on with hope and happiness in my mind. Rocky hills shelter me until the storm ceases and calmness surrounds me. (Christine, aged 10.)

Shades of T. S. Eliot's 'Journey of the Magi' here; this poem was read to the class; influences, too, from the movement lessons. The 'bardic' sentence at the end is all her own, as indeed is the sequence and structure of the passage.

About this time, the teacher decided to prepare a version of 'Ben Hur' in mime, dance and words, to be given as a performance to the rest of the school at Christmas.

After discussion the class felt that the 'March to Calvary' and crucifixion sequence must be included. The boy chosen to play Christ insisted on dragging a heavy PE beam around at every rehearsal. After one or two rehearsals, the children were so moved by and involved in this scene that their writing reflected this:

Jeering of the stalwart Roman soldiers arose for a stumbling figure staggering with his back bent nearly double at the weight of the cruel cross across his red raw back. He was dragging his feet that were cut and bruised, up the beginning of the pebble-stoned pathway. His knees were bent through the weight on his back. . . . Then he stumbled over a pile of rubble. He was sad and seemed in deep thought and as his body passed me I felt a quiver of pitiness. . . . Bitterness besieged me. I went away not wanting to see any more and trying to hold back my tears of sorrow.
(Michael, aged 10.)

Our Activities in the hall complemented those in the class-room; mimes in the hall reinforced and enhanced paintings and descriptive writing. Models of Roman galleys and chariots 'clothed' the mimes done without any scenery.

This project was very much a class affair. Most of the activities were class activities. They shared the experience.

When the time came to put on the performance, illustrative material, children's paintings, models and writing from the display in the classroom were moved to a corridor outside the hall, so that other children in the school could see them. The performance itself consisted of the mimes linked by music from the recording and children's own descriptive writing read by the authors. These were taped beforehand; the authors were also taking part in the mimes. Children had made costumes at home.

By the time the performance reached 'The March to Calvary' the hall had become Jerusalem and time had slipped away. It was one of those rare moments when the historical environment was as real as the present.

Sources of information

Books about Snow

ADLER, I., *Water in Your Life* and *Weather in Your Life*, Dobson (J/T).
ASTON, O., *Water*, Evans (J).
BARKER, R. S., *Water* (Study Books), Bodley Head (J).
BETHERS, R., *What Happens in the Sky?*, Blackie (I/J).
BRANLEY, F., *Icebergs*, A. and C. Black (J).
GIBSON, G. H., *About Our Weather*, Muller (J/T).
GAGG, J. C., *Water*, Blackwell (J).
PODENDORF, I., *Water Experiments* and *Weather Experiments*, Muller (J).
JOHNSON, E., *Winter Book*, Blackwell (J).
PURTON, R. W., *Outdoor Things for Lively Youngsters*, Cassell (J).
SHEEHAN, A., *Weather* (First Library), Macdonald (J).
WYLER, R., *First Book of Weather*, Watts (J).

Stories

GRAHAME, KENNETH, *The Wind in the Willows*, Penguin.
LEWIS, C. S., *The Lion, the Witch and the Wardrobe*, Penguin.
MILNE, A. A., 'In Which Pooh and Piglet Go Hunting and Nearly Catch a Woozle' from *Winnie the Pooh*, and *The House at Pooh Corner*, Methuen.
MOWAT, F., *People of the Deer*, Michael Joseph (J).
RANSOME, A., *Winter Holiday*, Cape (J).
TRADITIONAL, 'The Snow Queen'.

Poems

CANE, M., 'Snow Towards Evening' *Poetry Quest* (Magic Question —Magic Answer), Blackie.

COATSWORTH, E., 'On a Night of Snow', ibid.

HARDY, THOMAS, 'Snow in the Suburbs', *Collected Poems*, Macmillan.

ORLEANS, I., 'Water has no Colour', *Poetry Quest* (Magic Question —Magic Answer), Blackie.

STEPHENS, J., 'White Fields', *Time for Poetry Book II*, E. J. Arnold.

SWENSON, M., 'The Cat and the Weather', *Junior Voices II*, Penguin.

TODD, B. E., 'The Calendar' *Time for Poetry Book II*, E. J. Arnold.

Filmstrips

'Life in the Winter' (B417) from Common Ground Filmstrips, Longman Group Ltd.

Books about Metamorphosis

ABISH, R., *Butterflies*, Watts (J).

BLACKWOOD, P., ed. *Ants and Bees*, Transworld (I/J).

DEERING, H., *A Bee is Born*, Oak Tree Press (I/J).

HIRONS, M. J. D., *Insect Life of Farm and Garden*, Blandford (J/T).

HYDE, G. E., *British Insects*, A. and C. Black (J/T).

LEWELLEN, J., *Honeybees*, Muller (J).

LINSSEN, ?., *Observer's Book of British Insects*, Warne (J/T).

MANNING, S., *Butterflies, Moths and other Insects*, Ladybird (I/J).

PRIOR, M., *Insects*, A. and C. Black (J/T).

SILVERSTEIN, A. and SILVERSTEIN, V., *The Magic Change: Metamorphosis*, Blackie (J/T).

WHITELEY, D., *Insects* (Clue Books), Oxford University Press (J).

Stories

CARLE, E., *The Very Hungry Caterpillar*, Hamish Hamilton (I).

KINGSLEY, CHARLES, 'Tom and the Dragonfly Nymph', *The Water Babies*.

VON FRISCH, K., *The Dancing Bees*, Methuen (J).

Poems

LEVERTOV, D., 'The Disclosure', *as large as alone*, Macmillan.

SWENSON, M., 'Was Worm', *Voices*, Penguin.

Music
VAUGHAN WILLIAMS, *The Wasps Overture*.

Filmstrips
'Life in the Summer' (Primary Biology Series B415), Common Ground Filmstrips, Longman Group Ltd.

Books about Ben Hur
BALL, B. M., *Journey to Bethlehem*, Pergamon (J).

BOUQUET, A. C., *Everyday Life in New Testament Times*, Batsford (J/T).

BURRELL, R. E., *The Romans and their World*, Wheaton (J/T).

COWELL, F. R., *Everyday Life in Ancient Rome*, Batsford (J/T).

CRABB, E. W., *Living in New Testament Days*, E. J. Arnold (J).

ERDOES, R., *Picture History of Ancient Rome*, Batsford (J/T).

GOWER, R., *Life in New Testament Times*, Ladybird (I/J).

OGILVIE, R., *The Ancient World*, Oxford University Press (J).

PROCTER, M. E., *The Three Wise Men*, Blandford (I).

ROBINSON, C. A., *Ancient Bible Lands*, Watts (J).

ROSTRON, H., *Animals, Beasts and Plants of the Bible*, Ladybird (I/J).

TAYLOR, B., ed. *Ancient Romans*, Brockhampton (J).

UNSTEAD, R. J., *Looking at Ancient History*, A. and C. Black (J).

WHITTLE, T., *Royal and Republican Rome*, Heinemann (J/T).

Stories
WALLACE, L., *Ben Hur* (extracts).

Poems
ELIOT, T. S., 'Journey of the Magi', *Selected Poems*, Faber.

15

Newspapers

The headmaster had decided in consultation with staff to use the Spring term in work on a school theme: 'Communications'. A staff meeting was held and the broad outlines of the project on this theme were determined (see diagram, p. 115). A Junior class of nine to eleven-year-olds of mixed ability was to cover printed communication. The teacher decided first on a survey of the daily newspapers. She made an order with the local newsagent to supply daily five of the leading newspapers.

The teacher's aim was to get children to look critically at the content of newspapers but as the children had had little experience in this field, she began with a mathematical survey.

The class of forty children was divided into five groups, each of which would work on the same newspaper for the extent of the project. The initial work was carried out under the teacher's direction on a class basis. To give the children an idea of the aspects she wanted them to consider, the teacher first instituted letter counts. Each child in the class making a count of letters in one verse of a hymn—the same hymn and the same verse for every child in the class. The children recorded their counts as block graphs and discussed the most frequently used letters and the least used letters. The results of their count seemed to agree with the constituents of boxes of metal type supplied to amateur printers (a catalogue of these was available in the classroom). The children then took columns of equal size from the pages of the newspapers and made similar counts. In general, these showed numbers of letters appearing in the same proportions as in the control count. Where large differences occurred these were discussed at length and the words used and the content of the passages examined to see if this had any bearing on the letter counts.

More mathematics came from examinations of the alphabets used in newspapers. Most newspapers used three or four on any one page. Different alphabets were distinguished by the size and shape of key letters 'O' and 'X' in upper and lower case. Some key letters fit into squares, some into wide oblongs and some into tall oblongs. Measurement of individual letters gave children the 'points' used: 72-point letters were one inch high, 36-point letters were half an inch high and so on*. In this way the children had practice in using small units of linear measurement. The standard width of a column was also discovered and the children investigated when and why double columns and boxed columns were used.

The children also made counts of split words and the competency of the compositor was assessed by how few split words there were in any one column.

The children, in groups, also conducted an investigation into the greatest distance at which any front page headline could be read and they discussed whether the kind of alphabet used made any difference to the legibility of headlines at distance.

When the children had examined the newspapers under consideration in a statistical way, the teacher suggested that they should look at the indications of the kind of readership the newspaper might attract. This work had a mathematical bias as well as a sociological one. The groups picked out the largest front page headline of one issue, the front page eye-catcher (distinguished by its potential to attract people to buy the newspaper from a newsstand), the number and type of advertisements and to whom they might be geared (businessmen, housewives, families, rich people, bargain-hunters, men only, women only), the amount of coverage given to sport and the types of sport covered, the amount of coverage given to world news and home news, financial affairs and domestic affairs.

* This information would need to be checked for any subsequent work in light of metrication.

For some time the children wrestled with the problem of how to show these findings diagrammatically. The class had done some work on grids earlier in the term and one group had the idea of drawing a grid mesh of one hundred units on transparent sheeting. None of the acetate sheeting available was in large enough pieces and so the teacher suggested cutting two pieces of transparent 'Contact' to the size of a page of each newspaper. The two pieces were then stuck together to make a fairly rigid durable sheet of transparent material.

To divide this sheet into one hundred equal units was not easy. It involved the children in complicated calculations because the length or breadth of a page of a newspaper does not divide easily by ten. This problem provided purposeful practice in decimal fractions and metric measurement.

The transparent sheets were then ruled horizontally and vertically to make the grid. The first ruling was done with spirit marker but a final ruling was scratched into the surface with the point of a compass. These lines were finer and more lasting.

The sheet could then be placed over a page of a newspaper and calculations made in terms of percentage of the page in the case of news item coverage, sports coverage, advertisements, cartoons and illustrations. The percentages per page for each area under investigation were then added together and divided by the number of pages in the newspaper, to give an average. The children recorded all their findings in these areas on a large chart

THE BIRMINGHAM MAIL	Average % of total text	% p.1	% p.2	% p.3	% p.4	% p.5	% p.6	p.
News coverage	39·5	80		72		31		
Sports coverage	8							
Advertisements	45·5	12	100	18	100	54	50	
Comic strips and cartoons	1·5						4	
Photographs for news and sports items	5·5	8		10		15		

Chart showing some of the statistical findings on one newspaper

divided into five columns, each column headed with the name of the newspaper, so that comparisons could be made easily.

Front-page headlines and eye-catchers were cut out and mounted underneath the statistical data. The headlines were first tested to find the greatest distance at which they could be read. Some newspapers did not have front page eye-catchers and the children discussed the reasons for this.

Each group offered a written assessment of the kind of readership each newspaper was designed to attract:

A lot of men buy the Daily Mirror because of the front-page eye-catcher and the advertisements are mainly for mothers and children. Men who bet turn to the Sports page and the man who is not interested in foreign news but only interested in national news buys the Daily Mirror. (Richard, aged 9 years)

The children then began to prepare their own newspaper on the lines described in the '1066 and all that' project (see pp. 81, 82). The newspaper was to be an issue dealing with a topical event, but after discussion it was decided that topical events might become 'untopical' before the newspaper was issued and an event in history was selected instead: 16 June, 1919 was selected as being the day after the Alcock-Brown flight across the Atlantic. Most of the research for this and other items that might be in a newspaper of the same date, was done by the children in spare time at school and at home.

In order that the children should appreciate some of the processes behind producing print, the teacher set up a one-day project on the theme of 'Printing'. This was held during the project on newspapers, but on this day all the children's energies and thought were focused on the process of printing. The day was planned out as follows:

9.30 a.m. to 10.30 a.m. Exploration of the nature of printing. The children, working in small groups, were given a variety of material. The assignment for each child was to make a 'block' that would print a design more than once, and to experiment with the best printing medium and surface of paper to use with the block. The results were many and ingenious. Children made blocks by wrapping string around a cube of balsa wood, incising patterns in plasticene, pasting layers of paper cut in different shapes over one another. Some returned to the old tried method of using potatoes, others printed with hanks of embroidery cotton and balls of string. Some made leaf prints, prints from paper doileys and prints from bread rolls, sprouts and onions, cut in half. The teacher asked them to examine the relationship between the block and the print. The children's explorations also revealed the problems of choosing a printing medium which would be fairly fluid but which would not dry too quickly. Writing ink was found to be too runny, PVC paint too thick until it was diluted. The surface of the paper, it was discovered, had to be fairly absorbent (but not as absorbent as blotting paper or paper handkerchiefs) if a clear print was to be obtained. The children also found that the amount of pressure applied to the block during the printing had to be fairly strong and that pressure had to be evenly distributed over the whole block. Thus most of the problems confronting a printer were rediscovered during the exploration.

The children mounted their prints on the wall display with the blocks, that had made them, nearby.

11 a.m. to 12 noon. The class conducted a 'Which?' survey into papers. Four groups were given a selection of papers, shiny papers, tissue paper, school writing paper, cartridge paper, brown wrapping paper, blotting paper, paper handkerchiefs, cellophane, and newsprint. Each group tested this selection in a different way.

Group One investigated the absorbency of the different papers by dropping blots of Indian ink (from an eye-dropper) on to the surface of each and recording the results. Other media were used: powder paint mixed thick with water, school writing ink, printer's ink, plain water, olive oil and vinegar.

Group Two tested the durability of the papers and recorded the results when each sample was crumpled hard in the hand, scored with a bone folder, scored with a pin, pulled sharply, rubbed for a timed interval with an eraser, marked with a pencil, or with a pen.

Group Three took the same media as Group One and having made blots on the papers with each of these, observed what happened when each kind of paper so marked, was immersed in water. Two observations were concentrated on here: what happened to the blot and what happened to the paper.

Group Four tested the reaction of different papers to immersion in water, acid (vinegar), alkali (bleach) and oil (cooking oil).

Group Five had a rather different brief. They were given a selection of papers of different colours and surfaces. They were asked to write the same legend in inks of different colours (magic markers were used) on each sample and colour of paper. They then tested the legibility of the legend by measuring the distance from which it could still be read. This test was not wholly conclusive because children were not objective in their observations. They knew what the legend was and could therefore 'read' it without seeing it clearly, but certain observations were made, for instance where shiny papers could be induced to take a mark from a pen, the light reflected from the paper made the legend difficult to read. The children in this group agreed generally that black on white, black on yellow and yellow or white on black were the most satisfactory combinations from the point of view of clarity, and that papers with a matt surface were best to use.

A scribe from each of the groups recorded the findings of the group and these were mounted, with examples of the results of some of the tests, so that during the dinner break other children could see what had been done and make some assessment of the results.

Afternoon. Fifteen minutes in the afternoon was given to more general discussion about these tests. Then from 1.45 p.m. to 2.45 p.m. the headmaster, an amateur printer, demonstrated to the children the setting up of movable type and other principles involved in printing type.

After the afternoon playtime, the children were given work cards, one card between two children. The work cards ranged over the whole area investigated that day, for example:

Take a sheet of wallpaper and show the extent of the original block which produced the pattern.
Test the paper of an actual newspaper in the ways in which paper was tested earlier.

Find an example of one alphabet used in a newspaper article and show the relationship between the upper case and lower case letters, and between the width of the letters and the spaces between words.

Find an address of a paper-making firm and write to them asking for further information about various kinds of paper. (This letter resulted in a very satisfactory response from Reed Paper Group Ltd., who sent examples of the many kinds of paper they produce, some illustrative pamphlets about paper-making and a film with its own commentary on a gramophone record. The film was clear, concise and in all ways excellent as a teaching aid.)

The following day was spent in recording what had been done the day before, reorganizing the displays to tell a coherent story, continuing with the production of the class newspaper and researching into books for more information about newspapers and printing.

Other activities, which were not followed by this particular class, but which would be profitable are: a visit to a printing works (large newspaper concerns are not anxious to have very young children, but some small jobbing printers may be amenable to visits from small groups), and a visit from a newspaper reporter or editor.

Sources of information

Books

BRADLEY, D., *The Newspaper: Its place in a Democracy*, Van Nostrand/Reinhold (T).

CAREY, D., *Printing Processes* and *The Story of Printing*, Ladybird (J).

DAVIS, DUFF-HART, *Behing the Scenes on a Newspaper*, Dent (J/T).

DEAN, F. E., *Paper*, Muller (J).

DELGADO, A., *Printing*, Wheaton (J/T).

EPSTEIN, S. and EPSTEIN, B., *Codes and Ciphers*, Watts (J).

FOOT, P. W. R., *The Story of Communications*, Pergamon (J/T).

GOSMAN, M., *How Writing Began*, Faber (J).

HUDSON, D., *The Boys' Book of the Press*, Burke (J/T).

KAY, F. G., *Printing*, J. Baker (J).

PAPAS, W., *The Press*, Oxford University Press (T).

RYDER, J., *Printing* (Study Book), Bodley Head (J).
SIDDLE, W. D., *The Story of Newspapers*, Ladybird (J).
SIMPSON, W., *About News and How it Travels*, Muller (J).
SPELLMAN, J. A., *Printing Works Like This*, Dent (J).
STEWART, D., *Paper*, Wheaton (J).
WILLIAMS, B., *Know About Newspapers*, Blackie (J/T).

Other material
Penguin Primary Project: Communications Unit for 7 to 11-year-olds: Keeping in Touch, Machines and Messages, Signs and Signals—booklets, plus records and Teacher's Handbook, Penguin.

Books about Patterns and Printing
CROSS, J., *Simple Printing Methods*, Muller (J).
ELAM, J., *Introducing Lino-cuts*, Batsford (J/T).
GILL, E., *An Essay on Typography*, Dent (T).
GREEN, P., *Introducing Surface Printing*, Batsford (T).
PROCTOR, R., *Principles of Pattern*, Van Nostrand/Reinhold (T).
ROWLAND, K., *Pattern and Shape*, Ginn (J/T).
SALDE, R., *Geometrical Patterns*, Faber (J/T).
SHIPPERLEE, J. A., *Your Book of Lino-cutting*, Faber (J/T).
TINGLE, R., *Let's Print*, Evans (J).
WEISS, H., *The Young Printmaker*, Kaye & Ward (J).

Filmstrips
Filmstrip on paper with teacher's notes from The Bowater Paper Corp, Bowater House, Knightsbridge, London SW1.
'Paper and its Products' and 'Mill on the Medway' from Reed Paper Group Ltd, Education Services Dept., PO Box 1EJ, Reed House, Piccadilly, London W1 (on free loan) together with booklet *Paper, material of a thousand uses*, wallchart and samples of paper and teacher's notes.

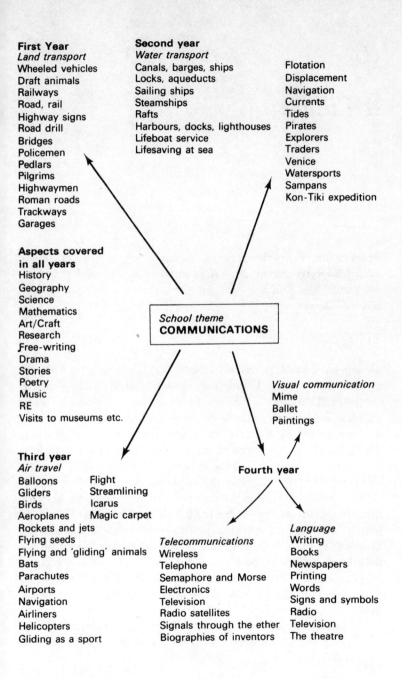

First Year
Land transport
Wheeled vehicles
Draft animals
Railways
Road, rail
Highway signs
Road drill
Bridges
Policemen
Pedlars
Pilgrims
Highwaymen
Roman roads
Trackways
Garages

Second year
Water transport
Canals, barges, ships
Locks, aqueducts
Sailing ships
Steamships
Rafts
Harbours, docks, lighthouses
Lifeboat service
Lifesaving at sea

Flotation
Displacement
Navigation
Currents
Tides
Pirates
Explorers
Traders
Venice
Watersports
Sampans
Kon-Tiki expedition

**Aspects covered
in all years**
History
Geography
Science
Mathematics
Art/Craft
Research
Free-writing
Drama
Stories
Poetry
Music
RE
Visits to museums etc.

School theme
COMMUNICATIONS

Visual communication
Mime
Ballet
Paintings

Third year
Air travel
Balloons
Gliders
Birds
Aeroplanes
Rockets and jets
Flying seeds
Flying and 'gliding' animals
Bats
Parachutes
Airports
Navigation
Airliners
Helicopters
Gliding as a sport

Flight
Streamlining
Icarus
Magic carpet

Fourth year

Telecommunications
Wireless
Telephone
Semaphore and Morse
Electronics
Television
Radio satellites
Signals through the ether
Biographies of inventors

Language
Writing
Books
Newspapers
Printing
Words
Signs and symbols
Radio
Television
The theatre

16

A Village

This is a direct experience project designed to give third or fourth year Juniors opportunities for original research, and practical work involving a variety of techniques. The spread of this project was as follows:

Mathematics

Measuring buildings, rivers, canals, locks, etc. with a view to making scale models. Estimations come first, and children can be encouraged to find a variety of methods for making linear measurements, such as using paces, using known measurements, e.g. the length of a brick, and testing these with instruments. There should be discussion about the best instrument for the job, for example, when is it best to use a foot rule, and when a surveyor's tape would reduce the margin of error. Children should be led on by discussion to discover the minimum number of measurements needed to be made: in regular shapes such as houses one length and one width measurement should be sufficient to make a ground plan. With more complicated buildings the children should be aided to see them as a series of regular shapes, or boxes fitted together. A rough drawing of the ground plan then divided up to show the shapes involved, will show what needs to be measured.

Finding heights of buildings can begin with estimations like comparing one's own height with the building, or counting the number of storeys, or by comparing a known height such as that of a door with the height of the building. Children may discover for themselves or may be helped to discover methods to find heights by triangulation either by using 45° angles, or by using a clinometer, or by comparing shadows with known lengths like the shadow of a yardstick. The children will have to solve many problems: learning to draw diagrams to give them a final answer, making sure, if they use the shadow method, that both shadow measurement of known height and shadow measurement of building are taken at the same time. Much of this the children will discover for themselves but judicious teaching will be needed to elucidate certain factors.

Having learnt to use triangulation as a method of finding heights, children will be ready to use a plane table and a 360° protractor to make panoramic surveys from the top of a hill or from the middle of a field. Panoramic surveys progress in accuracy. The first require simply sightings on landmarks without regard for distance, the second take sightings on near, far, and middle distance objects and these are plotted on a diagram as being within two circles, the near objects on the perimeter of the smaller circle, the far objects on the perimeter of the outer circle and middle distance objects between the two circles. Diagrams can be compared later with maps of the area, to establish the accuracy of the survey. The third method which can be used for making accurate ground plans of fields of fairly regular shape involves measurements from the plane table to each of the landmarks sighted. These can then be plotted to scale and a plan of the area made. Children can be led to make surveys using two points at each end of a baseline from the foregoing techniques.

The making of scale models should begin with the making of 'nets' based on the ground plan, drawing plans of walls on to this. The net can then be cut out and folded up to give a shape to which a roof can be added. The children should already have sketches, and sketch plans, and possibly photographs to help them with this. A preliminary discussion as to a suitable scale will also be needed.

In the field, according to the opportunities provided by the area under study, other mathematical surveys can be made e.g.:

The depth of a river at various points

Transects across streams or ditches (these can also be plotted for vegetation or soil variation)

The speed of currents in rivers

The volume of water in full locks

The descent of a canal

The gradient of a hill, or railway

Horizontal quadrats to show plant distribution, stone distribution (see diagram A.III), comparison between areas, e.g. cultivated and fallow.

Plant counts, taking a random sample

Worm counts

Weather study over a number of days or weeks

Temperature study, e.g. temperature under trees, in full sunlight, by water, on hills, in valleys, etc.

Bird counts

Traffic counts

Distribution of animals per acre on a farm

Milk yields

Crop yields

Population per square mile

A Natural Approach to Mathematics, Books 1 and 2 will help with some of the techniques involved. For other books see list, p. 136.

Geography

A preliminary study of maps of the area will help to place it geographically. Further panoramic surveys will support the map evidence. The contouring of a fairly compact area may be established by building up a clay or plasticine model of the declivities and heights from some central position in the field. These can later be compared with transects and with the maps of the area. A geological picture of the area can be built up by making a stone collection and a soil and subsoil study at various predetermined points. In the classroom the soils and powdered subsoils can be tested for acidity if shaken with distilled water and tested with litmus paper. The presence of limestone or chalk can be established by dropping weak acid (vinegar will do) on to stones. They should 'fizz' if limestone is present.

The investigations Junior children can make to help in the identification of soils and rocks can be charted as follows:

Colour   Texture   Leaves a stain on fingers   Easily powdered
Acid or alkaline   Dissolves in water   Dissolves in acid
Plants found growing on it
If soil, size, shape and type of pebbles found in it
Drainage of area where found
Suggested areas for soil and rock studies

Some idea of the commercial geography of a region may be obtained by establishing the kind of agriculture or mining which is carried on there. Traffic counts may lead to discoveries about the industry of the region. A visit to a farm, forest, or mine may be possible. Interviews with the inhabitants about what they can grow in their gardens are also helpful. Trees and plants also give clues to underlying soil conditions, and to some extent drainage and climatic conditions. A study of maps and then a return to observe in the field will establish watersheds and drainage systems. A survey of roads and paths will help to fix the topography of the region, especially when the paths are ancient ones.

History

The history of a region usually begins with the church and a visit to the church will be a starting point for historical discovery. Interviews with the vicar and verger will always be helpful. Do not forget that the churchyard will also give dates and other details which might lead to historical discovery. Preliminary lessons on methods of building will help children to identify and date houses and churches, provided they can distinguish the real from imitation. Local libraries will often help with reference material, books, maps, old drawings, photographs, etc. Class lessons to establish the wider history centred around the particular history of an area will help children to place their discoveries in context. Sooner or later time-charts can be made to give an overall picture. These will be more interesting if personalities can be included, e.g. if the area boasts an oldest inhabitant of great age the time chart could include the date when he or she was born and what was happening in the world at that time. Sometimes trees can be dated fairly accurately and a time chart could include an entry such as this: '*c.* 1066 Yew tree planted in churchyard of Saxon church. Norman invasion of England.' '*c.* 1415 men of village accompanied Henry V to France. Bows possibly made of yew wood from churchyard.'

Nature study

The natural history of an area falls into six categories: Plants, Birds, Mammals, Water creatures, Insects, Spiders. The presence of plants is linked to soil and drainage conditions and can be studied alongside Geography. If the visits are over an extended time the bird population may change, or the activities of birds may change. A chart of birds seen on each visit will quickly reveal newcomers to the area and the reasons for their appearance may be discussed. Town children are not always aware of bird song and records such as 'Songs of birds' (Ludwig Koch) can be played to the children before they make their visits. Children should always be reminded to respect the homes of wild creatures, and in particular not to disturb nesting birds by their attentions, and emphatically never to take eggs or destroy nests even old ones. Feathers will be found and a collection of primaries, secondaries and down feathers could lead to further study of birds.

The presence of mammals in a district is often only detected by their tracks and droppings. Children could learn to discover tracks and pathways regularly used by animals, e.g. badgers, to distinguish the spoor of a badger from that of a dog, or a fox, to distinguish between a rabbit's burrow and a fox's earth. Plaster casts can be made of some spoor, and it is particularly profitable to compare the cast made of a horse's hoof with that of a cow, or pig. Children will also collect hair and wool found on briars and barbed wire fences, and this may be identified. Bones are often found and a comparison between the bones of birds and small mammals may lead to interesting discoveries.

Pond dipping can be either a statistical study or an enjoyable form of observation. I find that Junior children are usually too excited about pond dipping to be very accurate in their statistical observations, but a profitable study of the numbers and types of snails in a pond was once undertaken by some Juniors. An aquarium should be made ready in the classroom to receive the specimens brought home alive. Care should be taken to isolate carnivorous species such as the Great Diving Beetle, dragonfly nymphs, and leeches. Specimens should never be kept in jam-jars for long. A large plastic bucket, lined with a large plastic bag is the best way of conveying water creatures and plants on a coach or train. Interviews with fishermen will establish the types of larger fish to be found in ponds, rivers and canals. The acquisition of a microscope especially of the binocular type will help to establish the types of microscopic animals and plants to be found in pond water. A study of plants growing in and around the pond should accompany pond dipping expeditions. A study of flying insects and larva too might be started. On one such expedition with a class of Juniors one group devoted their energies to studying 'young creatures'; this included caterpillars, tadpoles, caddis-worms, seedling trees, and fledglings.

A study of a small measured area, possibly within a horizontal or vertical quadrat, can include the insects and spiders living there. A fallen tree-trunk will show a different set of creatures from an area of living tree bark.

Children can also be encouraged to study spiders' webs and to identify types of web from the familiar wheel type to sheet and tunnel webs.

Preparation for field visits

The first consideration a teacher must give to organizing field visits is how much time can be given to it. A series of visits is usually more profitable than a single visit and so the area to be studied should be within a reasonable distance from the school. The finances are the next consideration, how much the transport will cost, how much of this can be borne by the children's parents and how much by the school. At the outset it is advisable to call

A DISK DIAGRAM
This shows a plot of ground in detail.

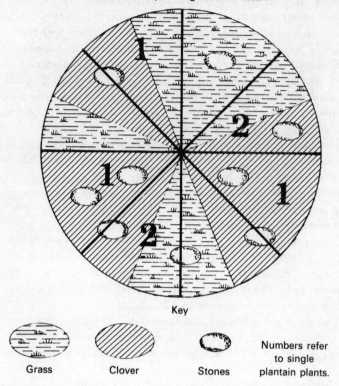

Key

| Grass | Clover | Stones | Numbers refer to single plantain plants. |

Procedure A PE hoop is placed on the plot of ground to be studied. The circle is divided off into eighths or smaller units by means of string stretched around pegs. This is drawn to scale on the recording paper. The plants to be plotted are then detailed on the drawing either as areas [estimated: e.g. grass covers one half (one third, one quarter, 25%, 20% etc.) of section] or as drawings (e.g. stones) or as numbers (e.g. plantain). These diagrams can be used: to compare one plot of land with another; to study plants on one plot of land at various times of year.

HORIZONTAL QUADRAT

This is another way of looking closely at a small patch of ground.

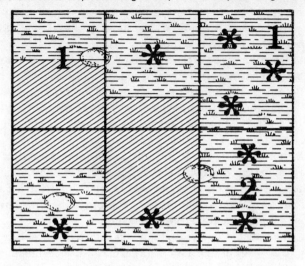

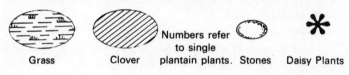

Grass　　Clover　　Numbers refer　Stones　Daisy Plants
　　　　　　　　　　to single
　　　　　　　　plantain plants.

Procedure Measure out a patch of ground 1 metre x 1 metre. Use string wound round pegs to mark this out and to divide it into smaller units. Draw this to scale on recording paper. Plot the growth as shown. A quadrat frame simplifies the marking out.
A Vertical quadrat can be set up against a tree. The use of a quadrat frame for this is recommended.

the parents in on the arrangements. They will often prove generous and helpful. Their permission will have to be obtained, in any case, if the visits lie outside the town or city boundaries. Tell parents what is required; the money, sandwiches, clothing, equipment the children will need.

The selection of the area depends on how much time you have, and how much experience of this type of work the children have had before. You need an area which has several interesting features in a compact region, where the children can work in safety, and where a base can be set up for equipment. Investigations must be made as to the owners of fields, and authorities to whom application must be made for permission to go round premises, to walk along canal banks, or to fish in stretches of a river.

The selection of an area can first be made by studying a map on as large a scale as available. Look for something with a nucleus, such as a church, a village green, a common, a hill.

Having selected an area, contact as quickly as possible people likely to be helpful and useful, the vicar, a local schoolmaster, a farmer, a landowner, a local historian, the verger, the sexton, the local policeman, etc.

It is always advisable to establish contact with a local school. Schools are often ready to play hosts to other schools, and can perhaps provide a room to store equipment, somewhere to shelter in bad weather, and lavatory accommodation. One cannot always rely on the coach which brought the children to be near at hand. Some coach companies prefer their coaches to return to the garage and come out again later to pick children up for the return journey.

On field studies I have made we have used variously a vicar's garage, a school outhouse, a cricket club pavilion, and a farm shed in which to store equipment and to find shelter in bad weather.

Contacts with people on the spot are always best made on a personal basis. The area must be visited in advance so that the teacher can have some idea of the possibilities presented by the area, and one can always arrange to visit some of the local folk at the same time.

Local libraries will often have books about their own area, and large central libraries in towns usually have facilities for copying maps and other documents that might be needed. A series of maps dating from as early as possible are useful to give the history in depth and for comparison.

The children should always be encouraged to acknowledge any help they have been given by people outside the school, and a letter of thanks from the class is always appreciated. We always made a practice of trying to attend at least one service in the church, and in presenting something the children had made, to the church and to the local school.

Farmers are very helpful, but it must be remembered that they are very busy people especially in the hay-making season and do not always have time to spend with parties of school children. There are some farms however which cater for visits from schools. There may be one in your area. There are also Nature Trails set up by the Forestry Commission in conjunction with Schools Rural Studies Groups, and it is worth finding out about these and the facilities they offer. Your Schools Rural Studies Association can help here.

Before children go on visits they must know what to expect and must have had some practice in the techniques they will need. The classroom displays put up before visits should show maps of the area on various scales, photographs and general information. Class lessons should direct children's attention to features they can observe, architecture, soil conditions, kinds of farming, roads, railways and canals.

Written English

If visits to an area take place over a number of weeks, which ideally they should do to gain the maximum benefit from the educational opportunities offered, the children should be encouraged to keep a personal diary of events. This diary should not be a mere record of activities but should reflect the child's own feelings and observations. Vivid and apt writing should be encouraged.

Further, all the activities should be fully documented and plans, models and graphs should be accompanied by written

explanations of how the statistics were obtained and what conclusions were drawn. All experiments should be described in
clear, precise prose, and a general form should be given thus:
Title of Experiment, Materials, What was done, What was
observed, Conclusions drawn, Supporting evidence from books,
or other observations.

Organization and equipment

Equipment needed at a field base:

Measuring rods of one and two metres. (These can be made by
children.)
At least one surveyor's tape
Measured chains—pieces of rope marked off in chains (or fractions
of kilometres)
Dressmaker's tapes
String and pegs for quadrats and a quadrat frame
Pegs for labelling finds
Clinometers, angle-finders, and 45° set squares.
At least one plane table and a large 360° protractor drawn on
hardboard big enough to fit the plane table exactly
Spirit levels
Compasses (directional)
Transect ropes—ropes marked off with tape or coloured wool at
10 cm intervals
Jam-jars, plastic bags, buckets and nets for pond dipping
Some test-tubes with corks for small specimens, also matchboxes
Squared paper, plain paper, large drawing paper (for rubbings)
Wax crayons, cobblers heel ball (for rubbings), spare pencils,
rulers
Toilet paper, paper towels, paper handkerchiefs, first-aid
equipment, drinking straws
Reference books
Wastepaper bins

We conveyed all our small equipment in a series of boxes like
ammunition boxes. Each box was labelled with the number and
sort of equipment it should contain so that equipment could be

collected easily at the end of the day. Every child had a box or piece of equipment to carry from the coach to the base and was responsible for seeing it was returned at the end of the day.

In addition each child should have a bag or satchel large enough to hold sandwiches, a plastic container of drink, a ruler, pencil, rubber, a pair of old scissors, plastic mac or sitter, a field notebook, a hardboard resting pad and a peg to hold loose papers to it.

The classroom should be so organized that, at the end of a day in the field, specimens can be laid out for further study, water creatures can be properly housed, and equipment stacked away easily. The walls should have space to take the children's recorded contributions and as the project progresses, the displays in the classroom should tell a clear story of the activities involved. In the classroom, too, there should be the usual work spaces for models, painting and for experiments, and plenty of reference material.

A field study built up in this way can make an interesting exhibition to show to parents at the end of the study. Children will act as guides to show visitors around the exhibition, and this can be regarded as an important and necessary part of their contribution.

Plans and assignments

If a series of visits to a village are undertaken the children must be given time, on the first visit, to explore the area and get over their initial excitement. It will be recognized that a departure from school routine is exciting, and we can trade on the intensity of that excitement to get vigorous and imaginative creative responses from the children. The first day's work therefore must allow for this. It is best to give the children some continuing activity to which they can return in spare moments. A tree study is useful; children individually can select a tree, and make measurements to determine its height, girth, spread, the average size of the leaves, its possible age. They can identify the tree, make a bark rubbing and describe it, makes notes about the tree over the time in the field, make a quadrat against its trunk, and study its ecology. A tree study can be started in the first week, and the time given to children to select a tree will also be time for them to explore the area.

A building study is another useful continuing study. Children working in pairs can select a building, take measurements that will lead to making a model, study its use, history, and architecture, interview its inhabitants (if any).

At some useful break in activity such as lunch time, the children can then be given assignments which they handle in small groups (I have found four to be the most manageable group).

NOTE ON RUBBINGS. Permission *must* be obtained from the vicar or rector of a church before rubbings are made of brasses or engraved stones inside a church. Sometimes the would-be 'rubber' is asked to pay for the privilege. Too much rubbing will damage the original.

Get children to identify tree at once from which they take a bark rubbing. Unless you are very clever at identifying a tree from the pattern of its bark it is easy to confuse rubbings afterwards. It is a good idea to ask children to make bark rubbings from several trees of the same kind and to compare the rubbings to see if a common pattern emerges.

Assignments given to similar groups of children in an area which contained a canal, a pasture, a lock-keeper's house, some wharves, several hedgerows, a church, churchyard, school and copse, were as follows:

1. Measure the width of the canal in three different ways (DO NOT SWIM).
2. Find the depth of water in Lock Four when it is full.
3. Make drawings of some of the plants growing in the walls of Lock Four. Try to identify them.
4. Find out what the workshops at the Wharf are used for. Try to interview some of the people who work there and discover their jobs and make drawings of some of the tools they use.
5. What is a dry dock? Is the dry dock at the Wharf dry?
6. Make sketches and take measurements of a butty or narrow-boat.
7. Make a collection of flowering plants growing near the water.

8. Make a collection of flowering plants growing near the hedge.
9. Make a collection of weeds growing on cultivated soil.
10. Collect, sketch or make notes of any evidence you find of mammals living in the pasture or churchyard.
11. Watch a tree or hedgerow for thirty minutes. Make a count of birds entering or leaving. Identify the birds.
12. Make rubbings of some of the dates on churchyard tombs. Back at school try and find out what famous world events happened in those years.
13. Make rubbings of three kinds of lettering on tombs.
14. Make a quadrat near the rabbit warren.
15. Make a quadrat on the canal bank.
16. Make quadrats in the pasture and on the path. Compare them for plant growth, etc.
17. Find the gradient of the path to the canal across the field.
18. How high is the church spire? Show in a diagram how you arrived at a result.
19. Make rubbings to show weathering on walls. Label your rubbings. Try and identify the material from which your rubbings have been taken.
20. Take soil samples from a path, a pasture, under a hedge, on the canal bank and compare the soil for drainage, texture, colour, staining, the plants which grow on each, the stones in the soil, worm population.
21. Make drawings of some of the windows in the church. Identify the styles. What do these tell you about the history of the church?
22. Make a panoramic survey from the centre of the pasture.
23. Make a count of buttercup plants in one square yard of the pasture. Make a daisy count. How do they compare? These are random samples. Do you think they give you a general idea of buttercup population and daisy population in the pasture?
24. Make a sketch map of the area. Back at school, compare your sketch map with an accurate map. How accurate were you? What would help you to be more accurate in your mapping?
25. Make a sketch of a fallen tree trunk, putting in details such as

fungi, beetle borings, etc. Try to identify some of the plants and creatures you find.

26. Make a sketch of the school. Try to interview one of the teachers, or children. How does the school, its building, organization and numbers of pupils compare with yours? Devise graphs and diagrams to show comparisons.

The foregoing are very general, but it will be seen that they give the children a broad picture of the opportunities presented by the area. Each assignment will also lead on to further study in depth. For instance, Card 3 could lead to a further study of plants without flowers, or to plants which grow where there is little or no soil, and to a general study of the link between plants and soil. Card 19 could lead to general study of erosion, or building materials. During the time back at school the children will be able to continue their researches and to consider ways of recording their discoveries (see Recording, below).

During the following weeks children may make more specific studies. These may be determined by the children's individual interests which will now begin to appear, or by opportunities revealed in the first week's study. A whole day may be spent inside the church, or down at the canal. A day may be given to visiting a farm. The farmer may talk to the children about the farm and suggest further visits. Some activity in the area may mean a change of plans. Hay-making may start and a day may be given to studying the process of harvesting crops, or to studying cereal plants. A fine day may be the time for a nature walk along the canal or river. A thatcher may start work. The opportunities will be endless and the teacher's only consideration will be which to pursue and which to leave. The decision must depend on the educational profit offered—opportunities for progressive teaching, and the children's serious interests.

Recording

Obviously where measurements have been made of a building a scale model is the best way to record the statistics. Procedure should be as that outlined in 'Mathematics'. Counts can be recorded as graphs or histograms. Collections should be labelled and accompanied by some explanatory text. Sketches can be turned into paintings or made into needlework pictures. For instance, a collage would profitably record the investigations of a fallen tree-trunk, and much discussion of textures and arrangement will enhance the original study and add vocabulary. Quadrats, once they have been made into diagrams, can also form the basis for needlework pictures.

Making a model of lock gates or level-crossing gates could lead on to a study of levers, and the ensuing models would reflect both an artistic, mathematical and scientific concern.

Collections of wild flowers, when pressed, should be arranged as attractively as possible and carefully labelled. Discussion about the attractive presentation of other collections can add dimension to the experience. A collection of feathers can be classified as primaries, secondaries, and down feathers and be stuck to the outline picture of a bird.

Maps and panoramic surveys need not be flat but can be modelled in three dimensions. Having drawn out a panoramic survey on a board, models of the landmarks used for sighting can be made and stuck to the plan.

As suggested in the section on 'Written English' the children's diaries will be written weekly. Each child should have a time to discuss his or her written entries with the teacher, and these can be polished and rewritten for inclusion in the wall display. No work that goes on the wall should have teacher's corrections on it. Work should be copied out and presented as well as possible by the children. Handwriting and the presentation that goes with it, is art work and a good piece of creative writing, or businesslike prose deserves a good setting, just as a good painting deserves a pleasant mount.

Where a particularly unusual or exciting experience has been shared by the class, this can be recorded in a class lesson as a painting or piece of writing. This gives a teacher a chance to continue to teach techniques while the atmosphere of sharing an experience is continued in the classroom. We were particularly interested in the bells of one church and we were in the belfry when the tenor bell struck twelve noon. Back in the classroom we continue to share this experience, first in collecting poems about bells, and reading them out, secondly hearing recordings of various peals, thirdly by sharing our individual impressions in class discussion, and fourthly by writing our individual records of the experience. Later we made music about bells.

Composing music to convey experiences is another way of recording. Simple rhythms can be played on percussion instruments, melodies can be devised using the pentatonic scale. After a village study children of one class put together the best of their written records on tape and music was written to link the spoken passages. The music was quickly devised by children working in groups in corners around the school (see page oo). The themes chosen by the children were: Busy Music, Water, Bells, The Solemn Church, A Hot Dreamy Day.

Collation

Collecting together the threads of this kind of study is best done in discussing the classroom display. Get children to act as guides to one another, and to other classes looking at the display. Later they can act as guides to visitors.

Sources of information

Books about Plants

ALTHEA, *All about Pines and Oaks and Things*, National Trust (J/T).

BENTHAM, G., *The Craft and Science of Vegetable Culture*, Blandford (J/T).

BULLA, C. R., *A Tree is a Plant*, A. and C. Black (I).

CHADWICK, P., *Wild Flowers*, Puffin (J).

COCHRANE, J., *Plants Without Flowers*, Macdonald (I/J).

DARLINGTON, A., *The World of a Tree*, Faber (J/T).

DEAN, J., *The First Book of Wild Flowers* and *The Second Book of Wild Flowers*, A. and C. Black (J).

DEMPSEY, M. and SHEEHAN, A., *Mushrooms and Toadstools*, Macdonald (I/J).

DOBBS, E., *Fungi for Fun*, Blackwell (J).

ENGELHARDT, M., *Pond Life*, Burke (T/J).

FITZGERALD, B. V., *British Wild Flowers*, Ladybird (J).

GREE, A., *Keith and Sally in the Woods*, Evans (J).

HYDE, G. E., *Berries and Fruits*, Warne (J).

JACKMAN, L., *Exploring the Hedgerow* and *Exploring the Woodland*, Evans (J).

JORDAN, H., *How a Seed Grows*, A. and C. Black (I/J).

LADYMAN, P., *About Flowering Plants*, Brockhampton (J).

MORRISON, R. and ROLLS, M., *Science in the Garden*, Blandford (J/T).

PERRY, G. A., *Plant Life*, Blandford (J/T).

PURTON, R., *Living Things for Lively Youngsters, More Living Things for Lively Youngsters, Outdoor Things for Lively Youngsters*, Cassell (J).

ROSE, F., *Observer's Book of Ferns* and *Observer's Book of Grass, Sedge and Rushes*, Warne (J/T).

ROSS, A., *Wild Flowers in Britain*, Blackwell (J).

SELSAM, M., *Plants that Heal, Things to Do with Seeds* and *Things to Do with Trees*, Chatto & Windus (J).

STOKOE, W. J., ed. *Observer's Book of Trees*, Warne (J/T).

WAKEFIELD, E. M., *Observer's Book of Common Fungi*, Warne (J/T).

WOOD, J. B., *Growing and Studying Trees*, Blandford (J/T).

Books about Spiders, Insects and Pond Life

ADRIAN, M., *The Garden Spider Spins to Eat*, World's Work (J).

BRANLEY, F., *The Listening Walk*, A. and C. Black (I/J).

CLEGG, J., *Insects*, Muller (J).

COOPER, E. K., *Insects and Plants*, Lutterworth Press (J).

DEMPSEY, M. and WATERS, F., *Insects*, Macdonald (J).

FICE, A. and SIMKISS, D., *An Aquarium* (We discover), E. J. Arnold (J).

GILLESPIE, T. H., *Our Friends the Spiders*, Chatto & Windus (J).

HIRONS, M. J. D., *Insect Life of Farm and Garden*, Blandford (J/T).

HYDE, G. E., *British Insects*, Warne (J).

KETTLEWELL, H. B. D., *Your Book of Butterflies and Moths*, Faber (J).

LADYMAN, P., *Grasshopper, Dragonfly and Daddy Long-legs, Ladybird Butterfly and Earwig* and *Water Boatman, Caddis-fly and Water Spider*, Methuen (I/J).

MANNING, S. A., *Butterflies, Moths and Other Insects*, Ladybird (J).

PODENDORF, I., *Spiders* (Junior True Book), Muller (J).

PRIOR, M., *Insects*, A. and C. Black (I/J).

ROSS, A., *Insects in Britain*, Blackwell (J).

SHEARER, V. and SMITH, A., *Butterflies*, Puffin (J).

STOKOE, W. J., ed. *Observer's Book of Butterflies* and *Observer's Book of Larger Moths*, Warne (J/T).

WHINRAY, J., *Pond and Marsh*, A. and C. Black (J).

Books about Birds
(See also list for 'Feathers and Flight', p. 35.)

BOWOOD, R. and NEWING, F., *Birds and how they live*, Ladybird (J).

GRANT WATSON, E. L., *What to Look for in Spring* and *What to Look for in Summer*, Ladybird (J).

STOKOE, W. J., ed. *Observer's Book of Birds*, Warne (J/T).

Books about Farming
(See also list for 'Cows and Milk', p. 15.)

ADAMS, H., *Farms and Farming*, Blackwell (J).

BOLGER, F. J., *Animal Husbandry*, Blandford (J/T).

CAREY, D., *Farm Machinery*, Ladybird (J).

HUGGETT, F., *Farming*, A. and C. Black (J).

JONES, D., *On the Farm Series* BBC (J/T).

LADYMAN, P., *About Farm Machines*, Brockhampton (J).

PERRY, G. A., ed. *Farmer's Crops* and *Farms and Farm Life*, Blandford (J/T).

WARBURTON, C., *Farming* (Study Books), Bodley Head (J).

Young Farmers publications from HMSO.

Publications about dairy farming from the National Dairy Council.

Publicity material about fruit and vegetables from the National Federation of Fruit and Potato Trades, Russell Chambers, Covent Garden, London WC2.

Books about Geology
ALLWARD, M., *Do you know about the earth?*, Collins (J).

BARKER, R. S., *The Land* (Study Books), Bodley Head (J).

BELL, G., *A Valley is Drowned* (What happens when), Oliver & Boyd (J).

DEMPSEY, M. and SHEEHAN, A., *Water* (First Library), Macdonald (J).

EVANS, I. O., *Observer's Book of Geology*, Warne (J/T).

MILBURN, D., *First Book of Geology*, Blackwell (J).

SHEPHERD, W., *Looking at the Landscape*, Dent (J/T).

Local geological maps are obtainable from HMSO and Ordnance Survey.

Books about Maps

(See also list after 'Houses', p. 27.)

BOLWELL, L. and LINES, C. J., *Using Local Maps* and *About Buildings and Scenery*, Ginn (J/T).

INGLEBY, T. and TAYLOR, J., *Maps for Mandy and Mark*, Longman (I/J).

SCOTT, N., *Understanding Maps*, Ladybird (J).

STORM, M., *Playing with Plans*, Longman (I/J).

Books about History

ADAMS, K., *Seeing History Series*, Angus & Robertson (J/T).

BELL, G., *A District is Born*, Oliver & Boyd (J).

BODMIN, S. R., *Village and Town*, Puffin (J).

BOWOOD, R., *Our Land in the Making* (2 books with filmstrips), Ladybird (J).

GRANT SCARFE, H., *As We Were Series*, Longman (J).

HUNT, P. J., *What to Look for Inside a Church* and *What to Look for Outside a Church*, Ladybird (J).

JACOBS, D., *Master Builders of the Middle Ages*, Cassell (J).

JONES, L. E., *Observer's Book of Old English Churches*, Warne (J/T).

LEACROFT, H. and LEACROFT, R., *Historic Houses of Great Britain*, Puffin (J/T).

MACKINNON, C., *Observer's Book of Heraldry*, Warne (J/T).

MIDDLETON, G. and MITCHELL, R., *Focus on History Series*, Longman (J).

REEVES, M., *Then and There Series*, Longman (J).

UNSTEAD, R. J., *Houses*, A. and C. Black (J).

Books about Transport

BAXTER, E., *Railways* (Study Books), Bodley Head (J).

BEALES, J., *Travel by Land*, Chatto & Windus (J).

BELL, G., *A By-pass is Built* and *An Airport is Enlarged*, Oliver & Boyd (J).

BOOTH, G., *Bus Stop*, I. Allan (J).

BOWOOD, R., *Story of Railways*, Ladybird (J).

CAREY, D., *The Locomotive: Diesel and Electric*, Ladybird (J).

COCKETT, M., *Roads and Travelling*, Blackwell (J).

DEMPSEY, M. and WATERS, F., *Railways*, Macdonald (J).

ELLACOTT, S. E., *Wheels on the Road*, Methuen (T/J).

GAGG, P., *Trains and Railways*, Blackwell (J).

JAMES, A., *Buses and Coaches*, Blackwell (J).

LUCAS, A. and LUCAS, D., *Lorries*, Methuen (J).

MIDDLETON, G., *Canals and Roads* (Study Books), Bodley Head (J).

MURPHY, J. S., *Railways: How they were built*, Oxford University Press (J/T).

REED, B., *Locomotives*, Pan Books (J).

SHARP, P., *Railway Stations* and *Roadmaking*, Methuen (J).

UNSTEAD, R. J., *Travel by Road Through the Ages*, A. and C. Black (J).

WYMER, N., *Roads*, Baker (J).

Books about Recording in Mathematics

BELL, S., *Pattern, Area and Perimeter* and *Scale Drawing and Surveying*, Longman (J).

MARSH, L. G., *Let's Discover Mathematics* Series, A. and C. Black (J).

RODDA, G., *Understanding Graphs and Statistics*, Nelson (J).

SEALEY, L., *The Story of Measurement*, Blackwell (J).

Other material

Bulletins of Environmental Education, Town and Country Planning Association, 17 Carlton House Terrace, London SW1 Y5AS (T).

GOODSELL, P. and JOLLY, B., Environmental Worksheets, Collins (J).

GOLDWYN, E. and HARRISON, P., Penguin Primary Project, Communications Unit (J).

Films

Environmental Studies for Schools from School Broadcasting Council, The Langham, Portland Place, London W1.

136

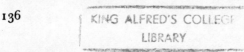